D1180023

IN SEARCH OF MAYA GLYPHS

IN
SEARCH
OF
MAYA
GLYPHS

From the Archaeological Journals
of Sylvanus G. Morley

Edited and with an Introduction by
Robert H. Lister and Florence C. Lister

MUSEUM OF NEW MEXICO PRESS

Copyright 1970 by the Museum of New Mexico Press
P.O. Box 2087, Santa Fe, New Mexico 87501
All rights reserved   Printed in the United States of America
Library of Congress Catalog Card Number 77-128565

PRELIMINARIES

To many laymen archaeology is a romantic escape from present reality. To them it seems that, with a minimum of stress, one simply mounts an expedition and bravely sallies forth to some exotic wilderness eventually to return—tan, robust, and bearded—laden with riches of another civilization, preferably of a material sort. Archaeologists themselves are sometimes caught up in this mystique of the bizarre, the remote, the fabulous.

The professional career of Sylvanus G. Morley did in fact have many of the qualities that more sedentary occupations lack. At a time when few persons in the United States or Europe had opportunity to travel to Latin America, Morley was penetrating regions there that were relatively unknown, decidedly different from the northern landscape, and therefore somewhat mysterious. His daily routine threw him into contact with colorful Indians or mestizos whose ways were at least interesting, if not totally strange, and the requirements of his research led him on a continuing travelogue adventure which, like many experiences, were more enjoyable once they were passed. The academic results of his labors were immense by any standards, for who could belittle the discoveries of dozens of impressive monuments of the past, some of them works of art even if not now completely comprehensible. Morley realized that others with more normal routines considered his life a fascinating existence about which they enjoyed hearing.

So from 1905, when he commenced his love affair with the Mayas and their history, until his death, Morley kept exceedingly detailed notes on all his activities while in the field. He drew upon this reservoir of anecdotes, accidents, thoughts, and exasperations to build a wide reputation as an entertaining storyteller and as a result became much in demand in both the parlor and the auditorium. But although he obviously was enamored with the dramatic potentialities of his out-of-the-ordinary way of life, Morley was a serious student and went to great pains to record every detail or observation about his findings that might be of any possible significance to other scholars.

At the time of his death there were thirty-nine volumes of these papers spanning the pioneer period in Maya archaeology. Morley's widow, Frances, gave them to Dr. A.V. Kidder, a close personal friend and superior in the Historical Division of the Carnegie Institution of Washington. Kidder in turn presented them to the American Philosophical Society for safekeeping in that institution's library in Philadelphia.

In 1963 the American Philosophical Society kindly voted a modest grant to enable us to prepare these journals for publication. The Committee on Research and Creative Work of the University of Colorado likewise provided some financial assistance. However, the sheer bulk of the collection of writings and their necessarily repetitive nature precluded any complete reproduction. Ultimately only portions of five journals were selected for this book, but we believe they offer the reader a rich flavoring of Morley's field experiences. At the same time they are representative of field operations being undertaken by a growing corps of scientists concerned with American prehistory. The wording is Morley's except in a few cases where there has been minor editing for more readability.

Robert H. Lister
Florence C. Lister

: vii :

MAP OF
A PORTION OF
THE MAYA AREA

MORLEY'S EXPEDITIONS
REFERRED TO IN TEXT:

1916 — o o o o o o o o

1918 — • • • • • • • • •

1920 — 𝆬𝆬𝆬𝆬𝆬𝆬𝆬𝆬𝆬

1921 — ▷▷▷▷▷▷▷

1932 — 〉〉〉〉〉〉〉〉〉〉〉

SCALE

MILES

| 0 | 25 | 50 | 75 | 100 |

| 0 | 40 | 80 | 120 | 160 |

KILOMETERS

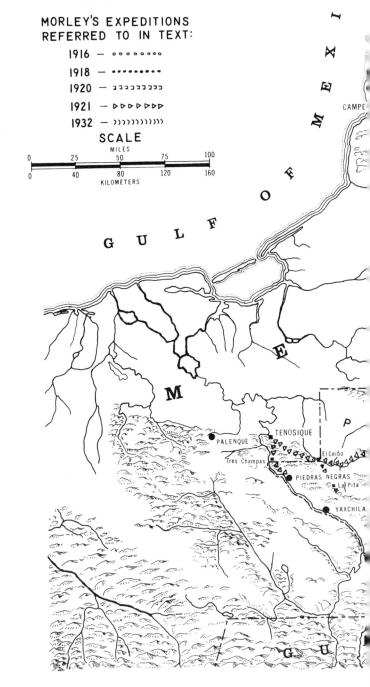

MERIDA

CHICHEN ITZA

O

TULUUM

Vigia
Chico

Ascension Bay

Santa
Cruz

CHAC MOOL

C

I

SEA

1918

AMANTUN

UL

LA HONRADEZ

XULTUN

Bejucal

UAXACTUN

Laguna

TIKAL

1920

Chunvis

CAYO

BENQUE VIEJO

Peten

TAYASAL

ES

BELIZE

1916

BRITISH HONDURAS

CARIBBEAN

Sylvanus Griswold Morley
1883-1948

INTRODUCTION

Today the Maya Indians are a heterogeneous group of tribes whose total population is in the neighborhood of two million. Although they dwell in varied physiographic provinces—ranging from dry thorny desert to dense tropical rain forest to high pine-clad mountain slopes—the Maya are unified by a basic linguistic stock, physical similarity, dependence upon swidden corn agriculture, and a past cultural florescence which is not now readily apparent in the humble thatch-roofed villages found in the Mexican states of Vera Cruz, Chiapas, Tabasco, Yucatán, Campeche, and Quintana Roo, and the republics of Guatemala, Honduras, and British Honduras. Not yet generally adopting Western dress, they wear brilliant woolens in the highlands, cool, loose-fitting cottons in the lowlands, and many excel in such cottage crafts as weaving and embroidery. Most of them have been acculturated through centuries of contact with Europeans, but some have been shielded from such intercourse by a terrain which does not invite penetration or a level of existence which does not promise profitable exploitation. As is usual in such cases of intrusion of one culture upon another, most change has been in the realm of the household and the *milpa*, or farm. Non-material aspects of life have stubbornly resisted modification. Modern Mayan religious practices, for example, are an intriguing synthesis of pagan and Christian beliefs with the former very close to the surface and the latter often so metamorphosed as to be unrecognizable by conventional standards.

The modern Maya have been known to Europeans since the fourth voyage of Columbus in 1502 when Maya traders were encountered in the Caribbean. A decade later survivors from a Spanish shipwreck were washed ashore in Yucatán, where they were killed in battle, sacrificed to pagan gods, or enslaved. The expeditions of Hernández de Cordoba (1517), Juan de Grijalva (1518), and Hernan Cortez (1519) sailed close enough along the shores of the Yucatán peninsula to allow the conquistadors to see pyramidal structures and mounds of dressed stones on the cliffs above the sea. They went ashore at some of these old ruins, which were already so dilapidated as to indicate great age, to erect a Christian cross on top of what they judged to have been a place of aboriginal worship. And everywhere they encountered the living Maya, they were met with open hostility.

As the Spanish armies subsequently penetrated the interior of the peninsula, they came upon larger, grander cities of dozens of mounds and structures swallowed up by a low, dense, scrub jungle. They assumed that these were the remains of former times of the peoples then occupying the region, although there were no such urban centers in use at the time of the arrival of the Europeans. At one ruined city was a vast *cenote,* or circular sinkhole, which the natives regarded as sacred. It was here, at Chichén Itzá, that Francisco de Montejo came in 1527 to encamp while he sought to subjugate the surrounding native populace. He was driven from the peninsula, but twenty years later his son returned to set up a military cantonment at another relic of the Maya past, the ruin of Tiho. Because of a fortuitous alliance with a ruling family, he was more successful than his father in permanently bringing the northern Maya under Spanish domination. His capital city of Merida was founded on top of other Maya remains. It was no easy victory for the Iberians, but it served to hasten the eradication of the Mayan past because zealots among the military and religious destroyed native documents and works of art. The Spaniards learned, however, that the ruins in the peninsula did in fact pertain to a Maya yesterday which had faded a long time previously, and they knew from personal experience that conflicts among the Maya themselves probably had accounted for the decline of that civilization. As for the Indians, their spirits were broken and they were victims of intertribal rivalries and European cruelty, but they continued to put up resistance until the end of the 1910-20 Mexican Revolution.

The Yucatán peninsula, whose terrain allowed for early conquest, also permitted such complete exploration that it was only a few years after the consummation of Spanish conquest in 1542 that all the major archaeological zones were discovered. However, they remained largely unreported to the outside world until the 1840's when two Americans, John L. Stephens and Frederick Catherwood, in the course of an extensive tour of the lands of the ancient Maya, hacked away the matted plant growth which crowded the flanks of the old cities, swung their hammocks across the doorways of dank, dung-covered cellular rooms, and set about drawing and describing the mute marvels that lay about them.

Several years after the Stephens-Catherwood visit, the entire state of Yucatán was embroiled in a bitter economic-racial strife called the Caste War. The regions adjacent to Chichén Itzá, Uxmal, Kabah, and other prominent ruins were scenes of vicious battles, making travel by foreigners extremely hazardous. Claude Joseph Desiré Charnay ventured into the area ten years after Stephens and made a return trip in 1880. Edward H. Thompson, a New Englander who came to Yucatán because of a position as American consul, found that his real interest was in exploring the ruins. In 1894, Thompson was able to acquire a hacienda which had been devastated during the Caste War but which conveniently encompassed the fabulous Chichén Itzá. Through him, Peabody Museum of Harvard University had an interest in the area because he gave specimens to that institution, there then being no Mexican laws which prevented the removal of antiquities from the country. With the rise of the *Pax Porfiriana* during the Díaz dictatorship, travel to Yucatán was made safe again, and most tourists seem to have made Uxmal and Chichén Itzá a part of their itineraries. However, Yucatán was relatively isolated from the rest of Mexico because of the lack of railroads and highways. The number of persons visiting there remained limited.

The Mayas who lived in the Guatemala highlands were more quickly put under the Spanish yoke than those who resided in Yucatán. In 1520 immediately after the fall of the Aztecs in the Valley of Mexico, Pedro de Alvarado fought his way southward from Tehuantepec to found the new province of Guatemala, subduing the native population as he went. No ruins of the sort to become known in Yucatán were reported as a result of this *entrada* for the simple reason that the highlands apparently had not supported the kind of pre-Hispanic culture which was characterized by the large impressive units of limestone structures.

The third major area of Maya occupation at the time of the arrival of the Spaniards was a vast jungle covered plain forming a wedge between Yucatán and the Guatemalan highlands. The many rivers and swamps and a fantastically profuse plant covering, added to a steaming climate and a faunal population of poisonous snakes, gnawing insects, howling monkeys, and treacherous jaguars, made these lowlands of Petén a forbidding region which was better avoided than explored. Nevertheless, the indomitable Cortez in 1524 and 1525 marched with one hundred forty Spanish soldiers and three thousand Indians, including the ousted Aztec leaders, through that clogged passageway to the narrows of Central America in what must be regarded as one of the most amazing, if not foolhardy, treks in the annals of exploration. He reported no Maya ruins although he passed near several, but he did meet the Itzá who had fled Chichén Itzá in the century before his arrival. The Itzá were dwelling then on a large inland lake deep in the heart of the Petén rain forest. Cortez is reported to have left a lame horse with them which they came to venerate as a saint.

In the next one hundred seventy years only a very few Europeans had reason to attempt to probe the Petén, those usually priests in search of souls to save or soldiers bent on capturing outlaw Indians. The Itzás, secure in their island fortress in the jungle, remained hostile to the Spaniards throughout this period. They were not brought to their knees until 1697. One of the parties sent against them in 1696 has the credit of reporting the first of the "lost cities" of the Petén, probably the old center of Yaxchilán on a cliff above the Usumacinta River which now forms part of the political boundary between Mexico and Guatemala. The island, or more likely peninsular, town of the Itzá became a *presidio* attached to the *audiencia* of Guatemala, and a few Europeans were assigned to its isolation. They seem not to have ventured beyond the clearing of their village, and ruins of ancient Maya dwelling places in the vicinity remained unknown, even to the Indians themselves. It was not until 1848 that a Guatemalan army officer happened upon the towering steep-sided pyramids of Tikal, only some thirty miles north of Lake Petén Itzá but as effectively buried by the jungle as if it lay underground. In a few years he was followed by an adventure-seeking Swiss doctor who removed a sculptured beam from the city and sent it to Switzerland, thus bringing Mayan antiquities to European attention.

About this same time the ancient center of Quiriguá, on what was to become the railroad route from the Guatemalan east coast to the highlands, was becoming known to a handful of travelers. Catherwood was one of them; he later reported that he was at the place for one day in 1840. Some drawings and accounts of the ruins were made but received little circulation.

Two sites on the northern and southern extremities of what was to be defined as the range of the classic lowland Maya were also known by this time. They were located in more open, accessible terrain. The city of Palenque, situated on a tableland in Tabasco, Mexico, had been discovered and mapped in the colonial period, but the records had been lost in the royal archives. A second expedition explored the city in 1786 but the overdue reports of that expedition were cancelled by the political storm brewing at the turn of the nineteenth century. The ruins themselves remained generally unknown in a remote out-of-the-way corner of the Spanish realm.

Far to the south, Copán had been explored, and even purchased, by Stephens and Catherwood during the 1840's. Although those travelers also rode north to Yucatán and then to Palenque, they never penetrated the Department of Petén, which time would show was the area of greatest Classic Maya occupation.

The first scientific exploration of the Petén was undertaken by an English nobleman, Sir Alfred P. Maudsley, who in seven different trips visited the three Petén cities then known on opposite poles of the area—Quiriguá on the south, Tikal in the central Petén, and Yaxchilán on the north—and in 1887 discovered a fourth which was named Ixkun. Maudsley is credited with the first serious attempt at decipherment of the strange looking glyphs found on the monuments at these old settlements. It was he who gave the name of Initial Series to the Classic Maya system of dating because he observed that a particular set of glyphs usually stand at the head of an inscription.

At this very same time Teobert Maler, an Austrian archaeologist, was undertaking explorations in the Petén. In 1898, 1899, and 1904 he carried out his work in the name of the Peabody Museum of Harvard University. His wanderings, more than any which had preceded him, considerably increased the number of known Mayan sites and indicated a sizable prehistoric utilization of lush lowlands which in modern days are virtually without human occupation.

Harvard had further interests in Maya archaeology, stemming from a visit to Yucatán in 1888 by the Peabody Museum's director, Charles P. Bowditch. Under Harvard sponsorship, four seasons from 1892 through 1895 were devoted to excavations at the extensive site of Copán on the southern limits of Mayan occupation.

As the tempo of exploration of the Maya area accelerated, so did interest in ancient New World manuscripts to be found in Europe. One of these was an abstract of a manuscript by the second bishop of Yucatán, Diego de Landa, who was responsible for most of the early destruction of Maya documents and codices but whose own writings about the Maya were most valuable in later research. He explained in some detail the system of writing which was still in use by the Maya priestly class at the time of the conquest. Apparently, it was an ideographic system that had filled voluminous parchment texts which the good bishop had burned. The hieroglyphic inscriptions upon the monuments of stone could not be so easily eradicated, nor were they plentiful in the northern ruins. Landa noted that they were concerned chiefly with but one thing: time. Time, it seemed, was of essence to the old Maya. Its passage in twenty, ten, and five year intervals frequently was chiseled upon columnar limestone shafts called *stelae.* Some, weighing many tons, were erected before temples and other important structures. Other texts dealing with time were sometimes placed upon buildings themselves. In order to interpret these date glyphs, it was therefore necessary to understand Maya calendrics.

By the late 1800's it was generally acknowledged that the ancient Maya had made remarkable intellectual achievements in the field of mathematics and astronomy. They had devised a vigesimal system of positional mathematics and were probably the first people in the world to arrive at the abstract concept of zero.

Numerals were expressed by three symbols: a dot for one, a bar for five, and a stylized shell for zero. In ordinary mathematical calculations, such as might have been used by merchants, numerals were placed in vertical columns. The first and lowest place had a value of one, the next above it the value of twenty, then 400, 8,000, and 160,000. A number written as follows had a value of 188,016:

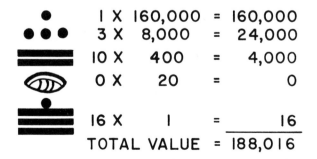

	1 X 160,000	=	160,000
	3 X 8,000	=	24,000
	10 X 400	=	4,000
	0 X 20	=	0
	16 X 1	=	16
	TOTAL VALUE	=	188,016

Small numbers did not require all five positions. The number 88, for example, used only the first two places and was written in the following manner:

$$\bullet\bullet\bullet\bullet \qquad 4 \times 20 = 80$$

$$\underline{\bullet\bullet\bullet} \qquad 8 \times 1 = \underline{\ \ 8}$$

$$\text{TOTAL VALUE} = 88$$

The major use to which Maya arithmetic was put, however, had to do with time. For calendrical purposes, the vigesimal system was slightly modified. The first place, or period of time, had a value of one (Maya term: *Kin*), the second a value of twenty (*Uinal*), but the third position *(Tun)* represented 360 instead of 400. This probably was done in order to recognize a unit of time approximating the length of a solar year. The fourth place had a value of 7,200 *(Katun)*, and the fifth 144,000 *(Baktun)*. Even larger periods of time, such as Great Cycles (2,880,000) were recognized, but are not important to this discussion.

In inscriptions, numbers were expressed in some instances by the bar and dot system and in other cases by stylized human heads known as head variants. Each of the numerals, zero through nineteen, was depicted by a distinctive type of head possessing its own essential characteristics.

In the course of a probable millenium of development, the Maya had formulated at least five different major systems of recording time, all carefully meshed together as cogs in a wheel, with dates so fixed that they could not recur for 374,000 years. As a starting point for their chronology, they apparently had selected a hypothetical point in what they called *Baktun 7* some 3,000 years prior to the first date they actually set down. Days were recorded from that mythical beginning in sets of inscriptions which Maudsley had called the Initial Series. It is now often termed the Long Count for it was a record of time which had elapsed from the end of the last Great Cycle to the then current year.

The most important element of the Maya calendar was a 260-day cycle formerly called by the Aztec word *Tonalamatl* but now identified by some as the Tzolkin, or simply the Sacred Almanac. It was a combination of thirteen numbers and a series of twenty named days which ran concurrently. The same combination of number and name would not recur until 260 days had elapsed. It was a ritualistic and sacred almanac which bore no known relation to any celestial phenomenon. The twenty days and the accompanying numbers were regarded as gods. The individual combinations of day names and numbers had great influence over the daily life of all the Maya. The luck of such combinations decided when ceremonies would be held, whether individuals would be suitably mated, when trading journeys should be started, and in general dominated practically every activity, whether of the group or of the individual.

The *Haab,* or solar calendar, regulated agricultural activities and the seasonal round of mundane affairs. It was divided into eighteen periods, commonly called months, of twenty days each and a closing period of five days. The sum of these (18x20+5) made up the calendar year, though the Maya apparently knew that the true length of the year exceeded this by about six hours. It formerly was believed that the priests, in whose hands such matters rested, corrected the calendar by additional calculations which showed just how many days the recorded year was ahead of the true year at any given time, but some Maya specialists now think that the Maya ignored this fraction of a day. This would have gradually put the months out of phase with the seasons.

The sacred almanac of 260 days and the year of 365 days were concurrent. A day was always identified in both time reckoning systems such as: 5 *Muluc* 17 *Ceh.* 5 (number) *Muluc* (day name) identified the day in the ritualistic almanac; 17 (number of day) *Ceh* (month) refers to the seventeenth day of the month *Ceh* in the solar year. 5 *Muluc* 17 *Ceh* would recur only after 52 years of 365 days had passed. This interval of 52 years is called the Calendar Round.

Initial Series texts on the monuments were prefaced by an introductory glyph which stood at the head of the inscription. There followed a series of five glyphs to be read from top to bottom, or if two columns were used from left to right and top to bottom. Each of these glyphs consisted of a numerical coefficient (0-19) and a period or value marker. The first, or top, glyph was the number of *baktuns* (144,000 days). It was followed by the number of *katuns* (7,200 days), *tuns* (360 days), *uinals* (20 days), and *kins* (1 day). This five place number was the long count of days which had elapsed from the point where the calendar began to the day referred to in the text. Next there were two glyphs identifying the day in a Calendar Round. These glyphs sometimes followed the Initial Series date, but frequently were separated from it by glyphs of other significance. The Calendar Round glyphs identify the day by number and name in the sacred almanac and by number of day and month in the year. The complete inscription thus identifies the day in both the 260-day cycle and the 365-day year which is reached after the number of days recorded in the Initial Series date have elapsed from the mythical starting point of their time recording system.

The schematic illustration, next page, shows a typical Initial Series inscription as it might appear in two forms. On the left, in a single column, the text consists of bar and dot numerals and normal form period glyphs; on the right, in two columns, the same inscription is depicted in head variant numerals in the first column and head variant period glyphs in the second. Both inscriptions conclude with a Calendar Round position which is in the same style as the Initial Series date. Note that the month *Cumhu* does not have a head variant form and is the same in both illustrations. Each inscription is preceded by a form of the introductory glyph. The whole text reads

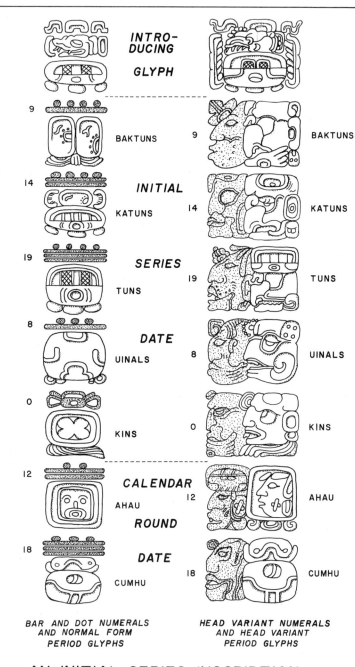

AN INITIAL SERIES INSCRIPTION
SCHEMATICALLY ILLUSTRATED IN TWO
FORMS

9.14.19.8.0 12 *Ahau* 18 *Cumhu*, in the standardized manner of reproducing dates in the printed form. 9.14.19.8.0 may be reduced to units according to values of period markers as follows:

9	Baktuns	=	9 x	144,000	=	1,296,000
14	Katuns	=	14 x	7,200	=	100,800
19	Tuns	=	19 x	360	=	6,840
8	Uinals	=	8 x	20	=	160
0	Kins	=	0 x	1	=	0

Total elapsed time = 1,403,800 days

Counting forward 1,403,800 days from the close of the last Great Cycle brings us to the position 12 *Ahau* 18 *Cumhu* in the Calendar Round. It is obvious that if dates were recorded in the Calendar Round system alone it would be impossible to determine in which Calendar Round they belonged, since dates were repeated every fifty two years. It would be as though the year 1967 were abbreviated to '67, which could be the 67th year in any century. By preceding the Calendar Round date by an Initial Series date the Maya made it possible to correctly place the day in their temporal continuum.

Other dates associated with monuments included a set called Secondary Series or Distance Numbers which tell one to count forward or backward by so many days from the base date. These bridge the interval from one Maya date to another by addition or subtraction. Generally a Distance Number follows the Initial Series date and leads to the next number, thereby avoiding the necessity of repeating the Initial Series for every date. They may be as little as a single day or they may span millennia. Also, there were Period Ending dates in the inscriptions which commemorated the endings of periods of time such as *tuns* or *katuns* or portions of such units. The significance of another numerical count of up to eight glyphs, called the Supplementary Series, was not apparent. Now it is called the Lunar Series and is known to deal with cycles of the moon.

Finally, as the classic cultures began to decline, the eight glyphs of the Initial Series apparently were deemed too troublesome to carve and were gradually replaced by an abbreviated version which has been labeled the Short Count or Katun Count. Dates recorded in that system might repeat themselves as frequently as every twenty years, hence have not been very helpful in unraveling Maya prehistory.

The complexities of these Maya time counts were first satisfactorily explained by a German, Ernest Förstemann, who did his original research in Europe on the several remaining Maya codices at the same time that Maudsley was describing Maya ruins and recording inscriptions in Mexico and Central America. He later extended his interests to the inscriptions on the stelae. The whole framework of the Maya calendar was elucidated by Förstemann and reported in a series of papers between 1880 and 1906. J.T. Goodman, a Nevada newspaperman, published an account of Maya inscriptions in 1897 based upon Maudsley's drawings of Maya stelae. Although Goodman made no acknowledgement of the work of Förstemann, and some believe his understanding of Maya calendrics was achieved independently, it is likely that he had knowledge of the German's discoveries. To his credit, however, Goodman did make some new finds relative to Maya hieroglyphics and his work has been extremely valuable to later students of the Maya.

Although these pioneer investigators deciphered most of the elements of the Initial Series, they did not understand its relationship to the Short Count nor was the Lunar Calendar appreciated. Furthermore, just how the Maya chronology corresponded to the Gregorian calendar was not determined. It was anticipated that the events known to have occurred at the time of the conquest could be related to others of an earlier period, and that these in turn could be keyed to the Maya system of date recording, so that ultimately one could work backward in time with an absolute chronology to the very beginnings of the Maya calendar. In fact, Goodman suggested a correlation of the Maya date of 11.16.0.0.0 with A.D. 1539, which was to be accepted by several later specialists and still later by most of the workers in the field. Few other prehistoric peoples with whom archaeologists had worked had been so thoughtful as to leave such markers behind them. The problem lay in their decipherment.

A quick appraisal of all the date glyphs known prior to 1900 showed that only one appeared earlier than *Baktun 9* in the Maya chronology and that did not occur on a stela. A jade celt, now called the Leyden Plate, had been picked up in 1864 near Puerto Barrios, Guatemala, which bore a date scholars interpreted as 8.14.3.1.12, or in the currently accepted correlation c. A.D. 320.

Thus by 1900 only the most meager outline of Maya development was known—that for some reason a rich civilization arose in the Guatemalan-Mexican tropics in an area now almost uninhabitable; that it spread out from some undetermined core eventually to extend north and south from Palenque to Copán and probably in its later stages moved northeast to Yucatán where it flourished after the Petén had been abandoned; that apparently, without central authority, it concentrated heavily on ceremonial structures and works of art which would have required massed efforts; that it survived by corn agriculture; that it evolved a remarkable system of arithmetic, astronomical observations, and writing which could not yet be fully understood by modern man; that the entire cultural elaboration disappeared long before the Spanish conquest, leaving only the basic subsistence pattern which was also followed by most of the non-Mayan peoples of Mesoamerica; that the modern Maya, because of uneven processes of acculturation, probably show more divergencies than did those of the past.

At the beginning of the twentieth century, then, the stage was set for a new generation of scholars to enter the Maya field, these men to receive what amounted to on-the-job training. American archaeology was still such a new discipline there was little accumulated data on the ancient peoples of the western hemisphere and there were few methodological guidelines to follow. For years Maya research had to remain largely a matter of arduous reconnaissance in order to learn just what kind and how many remains lay buried in the rain forests and what kind and how many date glyphs they contained.

One of those challenged by the opening up of Maya research was a young man named Sylvanus Griswold Morley. His was not an ordinary name, and its uniqueness was further heightened by the fact that it had also been bestowed upon an older cousin. The elder Sylvanus Griswold became a well known student of Spanish language and literature and preferred to sign his professional name S. Griswold Morley. The younger chose to be Sylvanus G. Morley, student of Maya culture and epigraphy. Friends of the latter further helped reduce the confusion arising from duplicate names by abbreviating the first name to Vay. It is Vay Morley and some of his detailed professional journals upon whom this volume focuses.

Vay Morley was born in June, 1883, the eldest of six children sired by an army colonel who was engaged in teaching chemistry at a small military college in Pennsylvania. His maternal grandfather, a Belgian, had taught languages at the same school. The academic atmosphere of this household no doubt had great influence upon young Vay, for even though much of his professional career was taken up with physical labors, it was those of the mind which provided the fuel.

When Vay was about ten years old, the family moved west to Buena Vista, Colorado, a new, raw Rocky Mountain community of a thousand inhabitants. The Colorado State Reformatory was located in Buena Vista, and the son and daughter of the warden soon became Vay's best friends. The youngsters were accustomed to spend idle afternoons in the prison library, where Vay first encountered the lengthy works of Hubert Howe Bancroft dealing with the history of various parts of Latin America. From them, the boy acquired a lively interest in that part of the hemisphere where later he was to become a legend.

When college time approached, Vay returned to the Pennsylvania Military College at Chester, where he devoted himself to technical courses, gaining experience in mathematics and reasoning which were to be put to use in a way which he did not then suspect. It is interesting to note that Vay's roommate at college from 1901 to 1903 was John Wetherill, whose family also had moved from Pennsylvania to Colorado. Some fourteen years previously John's older brother, Richard, had discovered ancient Pueblo ruins on the Mesa Verde of Colorado and had helped, through excavations there, at Chaco Canyon in New Mexico, and in southwestern Utah, to call attention to the rich archaeological heritage of the area. John later was to become a trader to the Navajo of Monument Valley in Arizona and a leading authority on the prehistoric ruins of that region.

Although in one of his first experiences at field archaeology Vay, together with A.V. Kidder, was responsible for some preliminary maps of several major ruins in the Mesa Verde area, there is no record that he was overly impressed by the Wetherill finds nor the prospects of a life of archaeological research on his home grounds. At that time it was the tremendously complex system of writing of the ancient Egyptians that had fired his imagination and appealed to his sense of appreciation for precise detail. And so upon graduation, with a B.S. degree in civil engineering, Vay transferred to Harvard to begin study under the eminent Egyptologist, George A. Reisner.

Charles Bowditch, acting as adviser to Morley, was not in favor of this plan of study. He sought to interest Morley in the relatively new field of American archaeology, particularly in regard to the undecipherable glyphs with which the Maya had embellished their most precious objects. He explained that the efforts of many scholars, both European and American, already had solved most of the mysteries of Egyptian hieroglyphic writing but that the known Mayan inscriptions which could be interpreted numbered less than half a hundred and without exception all pertained to the Mayan calendric system. A person who could learn to read the glyphs would bring himself lasting fame and would at the same time make a tremendous contribution to science. Morley, as an eager young scholar on the threshold of his career, could not resist that kind of appeal.

Another circumstance which was to lead Morley into Maya research was the advent of Alfred M. Tozzer into academic ranks. Tozzer had had four seasons' work (1902-1904) in Guatemala and southern Mexico among the primitive Lacandon, a Maya speaking tribe, and had made trips to various Maya ceremonial centers. He had a contagious enthusiasm for his research which he was to pass on to several generations of Harvard graduate students. An inspiring teacher, Tozzer was nevertheless a hard taskmaster and a stickler for detail, neither characteristic discouraging Morley, who in 1905 had the good fortune of being in Tozzer's first class of four students. He earned an "A" grade and acquired a lifetime direction. Thus, Tozzer and Bowditch together saw that Morley had the opportunity to make his first trip to Yucatán in 1907 to see the deteriorating but still magnificent Maya ruins and the modern descendents of their builders whom he had been reading about in a New England library. Among Vay's diaries is a series of four letters written to a favorite aunt describing this excursion, his brief map-making projects at Uxmal and Chichén Itzá, and his hopes for future archaeological work there. However, as it developed, Morley's first Maya research was to be among remains presumed to be older than those found in Yucatán.

In 1909, two years after this introduction to the Maya, Morley was selected to become one of a company of less than a dozen men with archaeological experience in this field. He joined two friends from New Mexico, Edgar L. Hewett and Jesse L. Nusbaum, to begin excavations at the site of Quiriguá in Guatemala, now believed to date in the last half of the eighth century. Because of its location in banana plantations belonging to the United Fruit Company, many travelers already had prowled through Quiriguá's plazas and had gazed at its dozen ponderous stone *stelae*—either standing erect as sentinels before sacred shrines or lying prone among the tangle of trees, lianas, and roots where they had been toppled by time and the numerous earthquakes which periodically rocked the region. But even though others had been there before him, Vay recorded a surging heady excitement at intellectual discoveries which were surely molding his future course. That same year, two of his Harvard associates, Professor Tozzer and R.E. Merwin, were nearby in the Petén district mapping the tremendous site of Tikal and visiting a half dozen previously unreported old cities hidden in the thick jungle.

At the end of this project, Morley rode on muleback for several days to reach Copán, a site with which he became closely identified and of which he would be made an honorary citizen. There he found that he was particularly interested in the numerous beautifully preserved monuments which possessed intricate panels of glyphs delicately carved in the stone, more of them known from here than from any other site. He knew for sure that even as interesting as excavation was, it was those mysterious glyphs, which reckoned Maya time back three thousand years, that utterly fascinated him. That year at Copán he began what was to become an encyclopedic compilation of inscriptions which he called his *Corpus Inscriptionum Mayarum*, the foundation stones of later epigraphic work by himself and a small group of equally interested men who hoped to solve their riddle.

In the spring of 1914, accompanied by H.J. Spinden and working for the School of American Archaeology of the Archaeological Institute of America, Morley spent three months traversing a thousand mile arc through the humid lowlands from Belize, British Honduras, on the Caribbean, north and west to Piedras Negras and Yaxchilán on the mighty Usumacinta River which flows into the Gulf of Mexico. This trip firmed his determination to find sponsorship for an ambitious plan of searching out, recording, and describing all possible remaining Maya date glyphs. It was a staggering task which he proposed because the terrain of the ancient Maya was still largely unmapped and generally known to be difficult, if not impossible, for travel. The Petén region in particular had the reputation of being a retreat for undesirable animals and human beings alike, with soaring temperatures, torrential rains, and a full blown civil war raging along the northern border. However, by 1915 Morley's epigraphic project had won the support of the Carnegie Institution of Washington, and the way was prepared for a systematic search throughout the region for ruins and glyphs.

The 1915 season Morley led the first of twenty annual Carnegie Central

American Expeditions into the Petén. At the end of the season he had deciphered glyphs at seven sites which previously had been undated. The old cities of La Honradez, Cancuen, Itsimte, Flores, Yaxha, Nakum, and Benque Viejo brought the number of Maya dated settlements to twenty-six.[1] Almost all the new dates observed that season were found to fall in a forty year period which apparently had witnessed the total decline of Maya civilization in the Petén. Furthermore, it was apparent that these latest Initial Series dates were localized in the northeastern corner of Guatemala.

Upon his return from this introductory trek, putting together historical events as they were known, dates that had been accumulated, and knowledge pooled from the work of several researchers, Morley formalized a Maya chronology for the benefit of the nineteenth International Congress of Americanists then meeting in Washington. This basic sequence proposed in 1915 stands today as fundamentally correct for the Classic Petén sites, but the day-for-day correlation of Maya and Christian dates he then suggested and the subsequent correlation of his friend, H.J. Spinden, was later rejected by Morley and most of his co-workers in the Maya field as being two and a half centuries too early.[2] And in the infancy of Maya research there were, of course, many lacunae yet to be filled by the dint of years of excavation and analysis. Neither he nor his associates were aware of an extensive formative horizon predating the rise of the Maya by several thousand years, nor were they ready to admit that Yucatán had shared the entire Maya cultural evolution.

After 1936, in general agreement with his colleagues, Morley felt that Maya civilization undoubtedly had evolved in the lowlands, perhaps as early as A.D. 300, and had flourished in many settlements, some known and some unquestionably still to be found under the dense plant covering, for approximately six centuries.[3] This long period, divided into several phases, Morley called Old Empire. It was the time when virtually all the dominant characteristics of Maya culture were developed—most unique of them being the corbelled arch and hieroglyphics—and when the population must have been one of the densest in the history of the world, perhaps numbering several million. Dated stelae, each one representing the labors of many craftsmen, were erected regularly at twenty, ten, and even five year intervals. Then about the beginning of the tenth century, for unknown reasons, the Old Empire of the southern lowlands faltered. Perhaps the collapse of the cultural pattern was due to social revolutions or to environmental factors, but certainly no more time markers were raised, though there was some evidence that the in-

---

[1]. Approximately eighty sites are presently known to have had carved stelae with date inscriptions.
[2]. The Goodman-Martinez Hernandez-Thompson correlation placing the Maya *Katun*-ending 11.16.0.0.0 13 *Ahau* 8 *Xul* as in the last half of A.D. 1539 is now generally accepted.
[3]. Current thinking places the coalescing of cultural elements which were to become lowland Maya civilization backward in time at least another millenium.

habitants of the centers tried to make periodic repairs to the structures which began to crumble around them. To Morley the old cities in the northernmost extension of the Petén must have witnessed the dying gasp of the Old Empire. The people concentrated there gradually dispersed, with the main shift being north to Yucatán.

Once in Yucatán, revitalized by a new environment and by contact with others, the Maya enjoyed a renaissance during the period from the tenth to the fourteenth centuries which Morley called the New Empire. Various regional changes in architecture were developed by the New Empire Maya, but some elaboration in architecture and crafts occurred because of the invasion of non-Mayan peoples. But to Morley the most puzzling aspect of the Yucatán occupation was the cessation of the custom of erecting stelae and a change, perhaps an abbreviation, of the hieroglyphic inscriptions for dates.

Neither Maya development had been a coalition under central authority such as the term "empire" implies. It was a city-state society throughout its various stages of development, but in the late phase in Yucatán an alliance of three major cities was attempted. The League of Mayapán, as it is now called, lasted for only two hundred years, during which time it probably rivaled the empire of the Aztecs which developed in central Mexico at about the same period. Ultimately, less than one hundred years before the Spanish conquest the League of Mayapán was pulled apart by internal dissension.

Insofar as the position of the Yucatán sites in Maya cultural history is concerned, Morley's reconstruction is now outdated. Since his death a very extensive Preclassic development there has been demonstrated, and numerous other sites indicate a large occupation throughout the entire Maya sequence from Classic times, contemporaneous with the Petén cities, to the Spanish conquest, and continuing today. In short, Yucatán is now known to have been continuously occupied first by non-Mayas and then Mayas for some three and a half millenia. The stelae erection custom and the involved Initial Series dating were Petén developments not shared by other Mayas dwelling in the Guatemala highlands or the Yucatán peninsula.

Two other fundamental concepts about the Maya which were generally supported by Morley and his colleagues are now being questioned. Morley firmly believed that the Maya had been responsible for the intellectual achievements in mathematics and astronomy which enabled them to develop complex calendrical systems. Based primarily upon archaeological investigations in the low, swampy coastal plain of southern Vera Cruz and Tabasco, Mexico, it is apparent that a powerful civilization known as the Olmec developed, reached a peak, and declined hundreds of years before Classic Maya culture emerged. There are also good reasons to believe that it was the Olmec who devised the elaborate Long Count calendar and invented writing.

Until recently the apparent obsession of the Maya with dating and the calendar has been explained as the work of priests calculating the positions of calendrical and celestial cycles in a religion which was basically the worship of time itself. Emerging from the recent studies of Maya writing, as well as their calendar systems, by such scholars as Eric Thompson, Heinrich Berlin, Tatiana Proskouriakoff, and the Russian, Knarosov, is another interpretation of this concern for recording dates. It is that the monumental inscriptions are of historical nature and deal with rulers, their families, dynasties of rulers, and the accomplishments of these individuals and groups. Some glyphs are thought to relate to contemporary historical events while others refer back to deified ancestors of a legendary epoch. It is further noted that such events as military victories and the relationship of one Maya center to another are depicted.

In the pursuit of the Maya glyphs, Vay Morley, during some forty years of field work, logged hundreds of miles in crossing and recrossing the realm of the ancient people. He is credited with the scientific discovery of several major sites as well as numbers of monuments and inscriptions. He contributed relatively little toward interpretation of the various kinds of glyphs appearing with those of the Initial Series, but he carefully published scores of scale drawings made under jungle conditions to provide others with the tools for study. In 1920 a huge volume on the inscriptions of Copán, which incorporated most of all the glyphs known to that time, was published, and this was followed in 1938 by a five volume work on the inscriptions known from the Petén. Without this tremendous contribution of the tedious, careful accumulation of raw data, our understanding of the ancient Maya would be limited. Morley's efforts thus must stand as a monument to perseverance and total dedication. Sometimes he traveled by canoe or on foot. Sometimes he rode alone with a company of native muleteers. He endured the countless hardships and monotony of the trail, the disappointments and frustrations of taxing explorations, the illnesses and physical discomforts associated with the tropics, and the local uprisings and brigandage. Even though he was not hardy and spoke atrocious Spanish, he developed a resigned adaptability which stemmed·from complete devotion to his work. If, at the end of the trail, covered with the slime of rotting vegetation or the encrustation of seepage on the limestone blocks, there was a single readable glyph, he jubilantly felt it was all worth the cost.

The second phase of Morley's career does not concern us here. It was taken up with administrative duties as director of a large scale Carnegie excavation program at the largest city of the New Empire, or Post-Classic period, Chichén Itzá, a research-in-depth project which his enthusiasm and diplomacy had made possible.

His 1916 discovery of Uaxactún culminated in a second Carnegie excavation program, this lasting twelve seasons, but Morley was not directly involved in that field work. During the 1930's Morley was absorbed with lectures and writings to popularize his chosen people, both ancient and modern. In 1947, after a thirty-three year association with the Carnegie Institution and exactly forty years of studying and living with the Maya,

Morley retired. He gave up his hacienda home in Yucatán which he had filled with Spanish colonial treasures, left a legion of friends from all walks of life scattered throughout Central America and Mexico, and moved to Santa Fe, New Mexico. There he assumed directorship of the Museum of New Mexico, an institution which had given him his first professional appointment when he had just graduated from Harvard. The following year he died at the age of sixty five, worn out by the rigors of season after season of tropical explorations, some of which are recounted in the pages to follow.

The selected journal passages quoted here vividly reveal this unique man. More than just the day-to-day accounts of life in the bush, they tell also of a pioneer era in American archaeology and of the painstaking, tough gathering of details which were to give substance to hypotheses for a new generation of students of the Maya past.

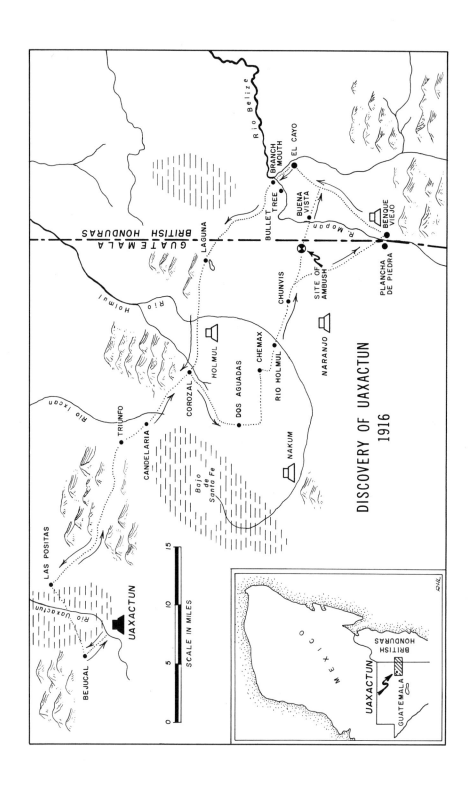

DISCOVERY OF UAXACTUN
1916

SCALE IN MILES

0   5   10   15

1916

DISCOVERY OF UAXACTÚN

Uaxactún is a very important ruin of the Classic Maya, located at an elevation of five hundred feet above the sea in dense Petén rain forest some eleven miles north of the larger city of Tikal and in the very center of the Yucatán Peninsula. Although it consists of eight main groups and dozens of smaller courts and structures, the site was unknown in modern times until a *chiclero* stumbled upon part of it in 1915. The following season he guided Morley there in what was to be known as the Second Central American Expedition. The journal passages to follow relate the scientific discovery of the principal structures arranged in three architectural complexes. Outlying groupings of buildings were encountered throughout the next decade.

Morley was back at Uaxactún during three subsequent treks, and finally in 1937 he viewed it from a low-flying airplane. It was through his initiative that the Carnegie Institution of Washington devoted twelve seasons (1926-1937) to excavation of the city, making it the most thoroughly known Classic Maya site until the 1950's when the University of Pennsylvania undertook a similar archaeological campaign at Tikal.

Uaxactún's importance stems from the fact that it was one of the most continuously occupied Maya sites yet known and presumably was near one core area where diverse cultural manifestations ultimately coalesced to flower into Maya civilization and where the custom of stela erection became most firmly entrenched. Together with Tikal, it has yielded more early dated monuments than any other site. One of its monuments also records one of the latest dates in the Petén, giving the site an impressive span of years from A.D. 328 (8.14.10.13.15) to A.D. 889 (10.3.0.0.0). In all, twenty-six stelae and three round altars at Uaxactún have date inscriptions. Furthermore, the walls of one structure were left in an unfinished state when the city was finally abandoned, indicating a resident population after cessation of stela erection. Likewise important is the fact that there has been uncovered a Preclassic horizon prior to that characterized by the stone stelae, towering stone-faced pyramids, and hieroglyphics, that carries occupation back an estimated six centuries before Christ and reveals the formative, perhaps "Olmec," stages which later culminated in the monumental architecture and sculpture. Thus, a probable period of use of some fifteen hundred years by an estimated population of upwards of twenty thousand persons is indicated. Excavations have produced one of the finest collections of Preclassic and Classic pottery, one of the oldest known painted wall murals of the Maya, and an apparently planned arrangement of buildings creating an astronomical observatory for determining the natural stations of the year.

In February, 1916, Morley and his group arrived at Puerto Barrios, Guatemala, on a boat from New Orleans. From there they proceeded by train to Guatemala City and then on horseback north through the highlands as far as Huehuetenango, where they were prevented from crossing into Mexico to visit some ruins in Chiapas because of revoluntionary skirmishes in the region. They retraced their route back to the Guatemalan capital and then on south to the huge Classic Maya ceremonial center of Copán in Honduras. After spending several weeks at Copán copying and photographing hieroglyphic inscriptions, they traveled northeast to the Caribbean port of Belize, British Honduras, where a small steamer was chartered to carry them north along the coast of the Yucatán Peninsula to the site of Tuluum and then back to Belize.

Finally by mid April, Morley—the archaeologist, A.W. Carpenter—the photographer, and Moise Lafleur—the doctor, accompanied by two Negro laborers, were ready to launch into the fourth phase of the work projected for the 1916 season. They went by boat up the Belize River to the interior trading center of El Cayo, situated at the head of navigation in the Petén rain forest near the border separating Guatemala from the crown colony of British Honduras. From this jumping-off place they planned to make their way northeastward deeper into the hinterland in the attempt to locate a newly reported ruin, later to be called Uaxactún, of which they had heard alluring tales. In less than three weeks the expedition was to come to a tragic conclusion. The recording of these events begins as the party departs from El Cayo.

April 25, Tuesday

Although everyone was up early, we made the usual late start, and even then there was delay. At the last moment, Jacinto Rodríguez said he had a horse he would rent, and also that he wanted $5 more. As he looked fairly honest, I loaned him this wherewithal, and he disappeared, agreeing to meet us either on the way to Branch Mouth or at the mouth itself. This came near to wrecking us before we had fairly started, since when we reached Branch Mouth, we found this festive flower had not yet shown up. Left Carpenter, Lafleur, and the two boys Andrew and Marius Silas, [servants] at the fork near the ford, and with José [muleteer] instituted a frantic search for Jacinto. Each grog shop was examined in turn, and after we had gone up and down the street twice, we located him in a semi-drunken condition. When reproached with his defection, he said he was ready to go, but his horse could not be found. Between us, we got him started. He said his baggage had gone ahead with the pack mules, but this later proved to be a lie.

We finally all reached the Branch Mouth and crossed. The pack animals had gone on ahead to Ojo de Agua where we were to sleep. We followed, leaving the Branch Mouth about noon.

At first the road leads over the valley plain for about a mile or a little more. The valley is covered with a dense growth of corozo palm, heavy black mud underneath filled even now, at the height of the dry season, with watery stretches. A narrow canyon with stony bottom leads into this, and before one realizes it, one is heading up a defile with precipitous sides. A mile of this brings one to a gentle slope, and a half mile of the latter to the foot of the hill. This chain runs roughly east and west and may be clearly seen from the Cayo itself. It seems to be the watershed which divides the waters of the Mopan-Belize river system from those of the Hondo-New River drainage areas.

A heavy rain caught us on the river plain, and, in spite of my poncho, I was moistened. Jacinto was very sad indeed. His hangover was stiff, and what with the heavy rain, his besotted condition, and prospective iniquity, he looked forlorn.

The hill must be over 500 feet, though hardly over 700. After reaching the top, there is still a league of indifferent going before one comes to Ojo de Agua.

All but two very indifferent *champas* were down, and it looked like rough weather. Each man set about making shelter for the night.

About five, José came to me and said, "Where is Jacinto?" Shouts brought forth no response, not even an echo. We were forced to conclude that he either was with the *arrieros* at the *ramonal* or had decamped. When the arrieros returned, the latter alternative proved to be the only tenable one. I was very angry and somewhat at a loss to know just what to do— whether to go on without him, bidding goodbye to the four stelae which he had promised to guide me to or whether to return to El Cayo and fetch him back. Indeed the decision proved to be too much for today, even though Carpenter and I argued back and forth until we were all sleepy. Finally— like most things in this country—it went over until tomorrow.

April 26, Wednesday

Rose about six and got the camp under way. Still I was undecided what course to pursue. However, by the time breakfast was over, it had gradually become clear to me that I should make the effort to locate Jacinto in El Cayo and bring him back with me. It was arranged, therefore, that I take José and go back for Jacinto while Carpenter should take the *mulada* on to Laguna, wait for me there tomorrow, where I would join him tomorrow night.

How these plans were broken wide open I will proceed to narrate. At Branch Mouth they told us that Jacinto had returned about five yesterday afternoon, badly moistened and saying the journey was not agreeable to him.

The first person whom I knew that we saw was Tía Chom, who said, "Have you no heard the news? The Mexicans took Plancha de Piedra early this morning!"

What incredible news indeed! I pushed into town to try to get more detailed information. The town was fairly buzzing with it. One could hear anything he wanted: that Emilio Guerra had been shot, that Laguna was already taken or about to be, that fifty mules loaded with thirty Winchesters and five thousand rounds of ammunition had been seized, and so on. There was little accurate information to be had. Everybody was worried and not a few downright scared. The District Commissioner had gone to Bullet Tree Falls to see whether the revolutionaries had crossed into the Colony [British Honduras] there.

Meanwhile, it was decidedly up to me to make a quick decision. If Laguna was not actually taken, it soon would be. No one was in doubt on that point. And there were Carpenter and Lafleur heading into it. There were but three courses open: either to go at once myself, send a messenger to call them back, or wait for further news tomorrow. There really was no alternative as I felt my place was with Carpenter and Lafleur without any further delay.

Jacinto had been overshadowed by more important matters, and I did not try to look further for the rascal. In the mean-time, José had come down with a hot fever and felt little enough like going back, but he went. He is, and will be, faithful.

Smith packed us a hurried lunch, and at 11:30 we were off. I made my further plans between Cayo and Branch Mouth. I decided that the de la Peña's oldest brother should return with us. His brothers were in the trouble as much as my friends, and his Spanish was far better than mine. When we arrived at the Branch, I put this issue to him squarely. He consented to go. We ate Smith's lunch, and at 12:30 were off. Soon we overtook Waight's drunken arriero and had his company until the top of the hill.

At first our plan was to have two ride and the third walk. This soon proved to be too slow. So José mounted behind me on the white horse, and thus we went to the foot of the hill, where we all dismounted.

We reached Ojo de Agua at 3 sharp, and after Augustín de la Peña and José had drunk, we pushed right on.

Unfortunately at this point we lost our way. José said our road led to Laguna but not via Chorro. In places it looked vaguely familiar to me. I soon remembered that Adams and I had come out from Laguna over this road last year. It led through a place called Kum. According to José's reckoning, we should have been at this place at 5:00, but it was almost an hour later when we finally got there.

Waight's mulada was already before us. I asked eagerly if they had seen any traces of the revolutionaries ahead of us. But according to them, everything was quiet.

It was now just 6:00. I figured another possible hour of light in the bush, with between 4 and 6 miles yet to go.

We tried another arrangement after leaving Kum. José, who knew the trail, went ahead on foot, and Augustín and I followed mounted. José struck a rapid gait, and in the first hour we put behind us some three and a half miles. Then suddenly the darkness literally engulfed us, and the bush became black. Soon in the welter of trails, each seeking firmer ground, we were lost. It was perilous riding too, because of the low hanging branches and *bejucos.* Fortunately José had brought some candles. With the light of these, we struggled on. Sometimes we had to turn back to pick up the hoof prints on our feeble trail. José's candle would flicker and falter and then sputter up into a weird burst of light that silhouetted his head against the trees. It was a scant half hour of this anxious roaming before José found the main trail, just at the southeastern end of the lake.

Now perhaps was the most anxious time of all. If the revolutionaries had taken Laguna, under what circumstances would we find our companions and how best to assist them? The plan we finally adopted was to extinguish our candle and approach the village quietly, intending to accost the first person we met.

Soon our anxiety was at rest, for on the edge of the village next to where our trail debouched from the bush, we saw Carpenter and Lafleur and the two de la Peña boys eating dinner. We gave a halloo and at last were with our friends after an anxious and trying day.

They had heard nothing of the Plancha trouble and were greatly excited. This excitement quickly communicated itself to the villagers, especially the city authorities, the alcalde and his second-in-command, who decided on the spot to run off to El Cayo in the morning.

Soon we were eating a good meal, the prospects of which scarcely a half hour before had appeared to me as distressingly remote. It was just 7:30 when we got in. We had been seven and a half hours from Branch Mouth.

After supper we made elaborate preparations against a possible night attack. We had six guns and two revolvers among us. Andrew and the youngest de la Peña boy had shotguns; the doctor and the other de la Peñas, Winchesters; Marius, the Lee [a rifle] ; Arthur Carpenter, the Luger; and I, my own Colt 38 automatic. What an imposing array of hardware! Andrew, Carpenter, Lafleur, and I slept outside the hut, the three de la Peñas and Marius within. Andrew, our arsenal inspector, gave every piece personal attention, and no doubt we could have repelled anything short of a German army corps. Fortunately, we didn't have to. About 10:00 all turned in with shooting irons convenient to hand.

April 27, Thursday

A peaceful night. No interruption of any sort. Woke between 4:00 and 5:00 and found everyone sleeping more or less noisily. Called Alfonso and soon the camp was astir. Four mules had strayed during the night. The arriero, in the meantime, had come down with fever. We began to ply him with the alkaloid pills and quinine. Ambrosio Martínez's brother lives here, and I did my best to persuade him to come on with us to show me the ruins near Santo Tomás, which his brother told me of in Cayo. I brought every pressure I could think of to bear upon him, but without avail. For some reason he wants to go into Cayo, and no offer of money or even my automatic could move him from this position. Ultimately the mules were found, and the work of packing began to go forward. Augustín de la Peña, as well as the city fathers, returned to Branch Mouth. The second-in-command stole a march on his superior and got off first. When the alcalde finally left, he fired four shots into the air, thus signalizing by a salvo of artillery his fall from power. He tearfully assured me last night that withdrawal to Cayo was his only course. Better life than the beggarly twenty per he was earning as alcalde of Laguna.

Presently we were under way. We were on the trail just three and a quarter hours to the Río Holmul, where we were obliged to stop for the night because there was no water for another four leagues.

It was very early, and we were going strong in spite of the usual mishaps of the road—cargo mules darting off into the bush unexpectedly or following wrong trails—but as there appeared to be no alternative, we stopped.

The country after leaving Laguna was low and only very gently rolling; no hills were crossed and only a few mounds and chultunes sighted, all, of course, being covered by a thick bush.

In the afternoon Carpenter and Lafleur went out hunting and returned with a hawk of some sort. Just before dinner Lafleur and I went down to the river for a bath. The insects gave us a hot time until we got ourselves lathered with the carbolic soap which drove them off.

The Holmul now is a series of shallow water holes, little like the roaring torrent that holds up muladas for thirty or forty days during the rainy season. One can cross it dry shod in many places.

April 28, Friday

An unfortunate delay. We were all up before 5:00, and Alfonso and Galileo off to the ramonal. About 7:00 they returned, reporting four mules missing! They commenced a weary search in which Alfonso, Galileo, Juan, Carpenter, Lafleur, and Andrew participated at one time or another. One party would come in perhaps with one mule, possibly with none. During one of these intervals of search, a really large mulada of twenty-two mules came by bringing a load of chicle out of the bush. They left this load and a watcher and returned whither they had come. At 10:40 Alfonso returned with the last mule, but then he insisted it was too late to go forward. I did not think so, but there was nothing else to do but bow to fate. Carpenter and Lafleur went out hunting several times but brought back nothing. In the late afternoon, however, Lafleur returned with a string of eight fish and two turtles, all of which we had for dinner.

April 29, Saturday
When the boys went to the ramonal this morning, they found one animal missing. In consequence we did not get off until nearly 9:00. At first the trail worked over a few low rises and then crossed the Holmul. The day was spent in crossing the valley of this stream. About forty-five minutes out we passed through what must have been an ancient town of not inconsiderable importance. Seven mounds were counted, one an acropolis fifty feet high and one hundred fifty feet square on top. Carpenter climbed this and reported the remains of a single building. There is a pyramid of almost equal height nearby.

Some two leagues out we entered a *bajo* which we were an hour in crossing. Judging from the rate we have been traveling, it must be about two miles long. These bajos, or bajiales as they are sometimes called, are depressing places in truth. Muddy under foot, low hanging vines, bejucos, and sweeping palms. One feels the presence of snakes and other creeping things without actually seeing them.

Finally emerging from the Slough of Despond, we were at the foot of a high hill on the northwestern side of the Holmul valley. There were a few abandoned champas at the base but no water. Through a break in the foliage at the top, we were able to catch a glimpse of the other side of the valley.

The hill we climbed today was between five hundred and seven hundred feet high. The whole top for a long distance back appeared to have been levelled off, and doubtless had been occupied. Noted two chultunes but no mound. Believe a thorough search of the crest of this hill would reveal a collection of mounds. Some distance back from the summit there was an aguada, evidently artificially constructed. The head of a small valley had been walled across and a reservoir made. Champas were built nearby.

Dropping off this range to a slightly lower level, we crossed another stony-bottomed bajo perhaps a mile wide, and ascending a low hill, were at our stopping place for a day.

Soon we were unpacked and everyone proceeded to his several pleasures. Again our valiant hunters went forth and again brought in nothing but a couple of scarlet crested woodpeckers.

April 30, Sunday
Made our earliest start, four hours after we had gotten up. We would have been off sooner had not Alfonso taken the occasion to mend all the *aparejos.* The trail was uninteresting enough, a good part of it over bajos

with stony bottoms. About one and a quarter to two leagues out our road led off to the south toward Corozal. One peculiar feature of the day's ride was the absence of mounds and chultunes.

Before reaching Triumfo, we passed a lagoon on the right, and a little further on came to the Jato de Candelaria. At the latter we crossed a dry water course. About a mile beyond we commenced to descend, and soon were at our journey's end at Triumfo. This was on the southeastern edge of another river called here the Triumfo. A close examination and comparison of my three different maps leads to the belief that it must be Booth's River, which later runs into the Hondo. The river was about like the Holmul and the champas half demolished.

Presently, as we were sitting around, who should come into the clearing but a man with a gun. Andrew and I were not slow in recognizing an old friend, the Tabascano who cooked bread for us on our trip to Nakum last year. He was looking after some chicle in the bush for Maldonado and was expecting a mulada at any moment. He brought a strange tale of a sick man in his champa, a poor devil who had been found in the bush further in and who was out of his head. The ill man had been with him some two months now and was getting weaker and weaker. He feared that if help did not come soon, he would die. Lafleur said he would go over after lunch.

Lafleur found the ill one on a bed of poles covered with a filthy blanket. Every breath was drawn with effort, and his face had a harried drawn look. Lafleur gave him a thorough examination, including a number of pressures, under all of which the poor devil shrieked dismally. With little hesitation, Lafleur pronounced the trouble as tertiary syphilis. He left some medicine and promised to return in the morning. The guard of the chicle was gratitude itself and offered Lafleur a prettily made little set of chairs and sofa all contrived out of cojolito feathers.

May 1, Monday

I had been speculating last evening and this morning as to the advisability of returning by way of Encanto in order to try to decipher the date on a stela Merwin [archaeologist working for the Peabody Museum of Harvard] found there. I sent José on over to the baker's jato to see if he could get any information. The baker could and did give me detailed information as to the location of the Encanto stela, so detailed in fact that I have about decided to return that way.

At 9:15 we bid goodbye to the sick man and his nurse and continued our journey.

The country is slightly hilly, covered with the same dense bush. We passed little of interest until just before our destination, when we crossed through a good sized group of mounds. Our destination turned out to be only three leagues from Triumfo, and though I objected vigorously at stopping here, was assured there was no water beyond this stop for another four leagues. Another trouble speedily presented itself. The water here was simply vile, filled with algae, and even in a small receptacle appeared green.

Moreover, the party was split, Andrew, Marius, Juan, and José not being here when we arrived. We shot off the Winchester; but it brought no response. After having coffee, Alfonso set out to look for the others. An hour later they all returned, reporting an excellent aguada. Alfonso, however, wouldn't reload. So we had to resort to the laborious expedient of carrying water from the other aguada. We brought back about six gallons, two of the canvas buckets being full.

José showed me a ruin near the aguada from which we brought the water. The wall was standing to a height of seven or eight feet. It was well laid and was composed of small pieces, like the Tikal masonry. I never see these memorials of a long forgotten people but that "sic fugit gloria mundi" comes to mind. Here they lie buried in an all but impenetrable bush, long forgotten of man, the very names of their builders unknown. What endeavor, what tremendous effort went into their construction, and all for naught. Now with vines creeping over their crumbling walls, massive trees rending their very foundations, these once holy places have become the haunts of wild beasts and are eloquent testimonials to the transitory character of mundane pomps and vanities.

We eliminated lunch and had a good dinner. Carpenter deserted the cot brigade for a hammock. As it looked like rain, Lafleur and I slept under a particularly snaky looking champa. Several times we heard the leaves overhead rustle, and vivid imaginations pictured writhing snakes poised over us. With these and other pleasant reflections and occupations, such as picking the *garrapatas* from each other, we turned in about 9:00.

May 2, Tuesday

Absolutely the worst day yet. To begin with, everybody woke up at sixes and sevens, perhaps because the garrapatas and fleas had given us an itchy miserable sort of night. Next Alfonso and Galileo were dissatisfied with Andrew's wheat flour tortillas, nor could I blame them on that score. To show their displeasure, they refused to eat anything, but instead went out with their gun to look for the missing mule. Lafleur went hunting and about 8:30 brought in the missing animal. I fired off three shots to summon the other searchers back to camp and then went to examine the group of ruins near to which we were camped.

This consisted of a number of mounds with perhaps a dozen of them being fairly large. The principal structure on the plaza faced south and rose from a couple of terraces, the lower one being the level on which the greater part of the other mound stood.

The other principal structure was one of the high temple type, which faced west. This must have towered at least one hundred twenty-five feet above the ground. There were no traces of its extensive masonry; however, part of the stairway was still preserved. Lafleur and I climbed this and succeeded in obtaining a fine view from the summit. The country around appears to be gently rolling.

Slipping and sliding down the steep mound sides, we reached the bottom in safety, and soon were back in camp, where everything was wrong.It was then 9:00, and according to the three arrieros, far too late to start today! They had brought in a *cojolito* and were about to cook it.

I put my foot down on that and insisted that we had to get off today. They were sullen and said they couldn't go without eating. So I had Andrew immediately prepare them a good meal. Even then they would have hung back if I hadn't pushed them. It was just five minutes past 10:00 when the last pack was finished, and we filed out of the clearing.

Meanwhile another annoyance began to make itself felt. During our archaeological peregrinations we had accumulated many seed ticks, and now with hosts of these swarming over our bodies, hiding in out-of-the-way corners of our clothes, we had a miserable time of it. . . .scratching here, clawing there, and cursing roundly.

But we were started, or thought we were. About a mile out, we heard someone off to our right cutting ramon. In another mile we came to the Jato de San Clemente where we should have passed the night. There was a chicle guard here, who reported very distressing conditions ahead. No water and long jornadas. It was then nearly eleven. Alfonso decided it was useless to go forward. I was furious as we had done only a half league. It was an hour until noon, and we were stopping. I protested vigorously, but he said it was impossible. I insisted that he had promised me that we would make Bejucal in two jornadas. He promised that we would. In eloquent terms he vowed he would put me in Bejucal tomorrow night, even if all his animals died on the road in so doing. I did not wish to kill his mules, but I most ardently desired to reach Bejucal, having been eight days on the road already. With this promise, however, I had to be satisfied.

During these heated discussions a mulada passed coming from El Cayo, the very first we had met since leaving. They left El Cayo three days after we did and brought the news that the rebels took Laguna Sunday, having abandoned Plancha. An hour later the owner of the mules arrived. He proved to be an old friend. Stopped overnight with him at Chunvis two years ago. He gave more details but no startling new features. He himself had lost three chicleros, three mules, saddles, and bridles. He reported a lot of loose animals in the bush, from muladas that had been captured and turned out, and he had appropriated one. On his return he intended to requisition two others to recompense him for what he had lost. I gave him some coffee, and he went on.

In the afternoon Carpenter and Lafleur went hunting, and I took a bath in the collapsible tub. This was the first time I had had occasion to use it, and it certainly proved its worth. It is light, compact, and serviceable, and if cleanliness is next to godliness, is certainly to be recommended as a powerful religious stimulant.

May 3, Wednesday

Awoke first at 11:00, then at 12:00, then at 1:00, and again at 3:00, when I called Alfonso. He in turn awakened Chon, and taking lanterns, the two of them set off for the ramonal, which they made all of a mile away.

At 4:00 I aroused Andrew, and at 4:30 we were all up. Presently, Alfonso and Chon were heard yodling the mules along, and soon they were being herded into the clearing. At first Alfonso reported all seventeen as present, but a recount disclosed only sixteen. Swearing roundly at the missing animal, Alfonso returned to the ramonal, and in due time brought it back. We who were going ahead saddled up first, and leaving final word to be sure and come through at all hazards, got off at twenty minutes before 6:00.

At half past 8:00 we passed the champas of Esperanza and exchanged a few words with the guard in charge. About two miles beyond this, the trail forked. We took the left one which bears west. The right is the main road for Las Palmas, San Blas, Santa Isabel, Carribal, San Miguel, and Santo Tomás, up to the Mexican line.

Another mile brought us to Las Positas, the place where we should have slept last night. There is a very good aguada here now. I left a note for the boys attached to one of the projecting poles of the champa, and we continued on our way. Up to this point the trail had been open and fairly good, bearing northwest or west.

From Las Positas on, however, the trail had not been used for two years. In consequence, it was blocked here and there by fallen trees. Chon cut these away. It was not long before we struck a large bajo, which in the rains must be a vast swamp. It took us just two hours to emerge from this melancholy tangle of bejucos, logwood, creepers, vines and rotting vegetations. On the far side there were a few champas but no water. Bejucal, Chon said, was a league beyond. Taking the only trail emerging from the clearing, we continued westward, leaving as early as 12:30. About an hour later I asked Chon if we were not nearly there, and he said we still had a half league to go. I thought this queer, but said nothing for another half hour. Then I asked the same question and got the same reply. It was painfully obvious that Chon was lost. I asked him so, and he said, "Who knows?" Whereupon I, at least, knew that we were.

Nothing could be done but return to try to pick up the lost trail. Chon seemed certain that as far as the champas on this side of the bajo we were in the right trail, and that our mistake was somewhere between the point where we now found ourselves and these champas. Here was a three hour loss. As I calculated the pack animals were not more than two hours behind us, it seemed as though they would take the right trail to Bejucal and get in before us.

It was just 2:00 when we turned about. At 3:00 some shouting in the bush ahead, cries, halloos, and the tinkling of a bell all advised that the mulada was approaching. Presently it came in sight, Alfonso in the lead. He at once wanted to know what was wrong, and learning, delivered a volley of oaths that would have pierced six-inch armor plate. Around he wheeled and disappeared.

There ensued tremendous confusion. In turning the mules back, some strayed into the bush. On all sides arose shouts and oaths. Cargoes crashed through the bush. Carpenter and Lafleur wanted to know what was afoot. More confusion. All became separated, each guarding some particularly obstinate cargo animal chance had thrown to his care. Proceeding in this disarticulate manner, in time we came to a right hand trail, about a half league from the champas we had passed on this side of the bajo. Alfonso had gone on ahead here.

The dartings hither and thither through the bush had loosened most of the cargoes, and these now had to be adjusted. I assisted Galileo with the camera pack until Chon came up. In this disconsolate manner, we continued on our way, José steadfastly failing to recognize the trail and raising an increasing gloom in all breasts. Late in the afternoon we passed some old ramonales and soon were at Bejucal.

There were a number of champas, a fairly good sized aguada, and a considerable clearing made on the site of an old plaza. José was very sad; his fever had returned, and he was quite ill. Chon also had a temperature. It rained hard. Food was getting low, and to cap this dismal climax, José did not seem sure that this was his Bejucal. My feelings can better be imagined than described.

We had gone close on to nine miles out of our way because of losing our trail, and I was well tired out. Physically and mentally worn, I retired early. Lafleur and Carpenter were not long behind me.

May 4, Thursday

It rained in the night and tried hard to do so in the day. José said he felt too ill to look up the ruins. It created an awkward situation. Our per diem is high, food low, and no work can go forward until the ruins are found. Lafleur doped José with a little strychnia, a little whiskey, and a little camphor monobromate. Under these and my moral suasion, we finally got him off. Lafleur accompanied him to keep him "in condition" and Alfonso went along to show the way to the champas of San Leandro, near which the ruins are said to be located.

They had scarcely gone before a shot was heard. José came back bringing a cojolito, which Alfonso had killed. Carpenter had found some honey and went out to get it. The camp settled down to quiet. I plotted up our dead reckoning. On my two available maps, I found out the startling fact that we are west of the Flores meridian, and not too far from Chuntuqui. I feel this may be an exaggeration of the distance we have covered and in my final map shall consider two miles an hour—in the straight line toward our final destination—about as much as we have done. In this way the morning slipped away. Chon came in with three birds, another cojolito, and two kambules.

Carpenter did not come for lunch. About 2:00, after he had been out for four hours, I began to be worried. I had Marius fire the Lee in the hope Carpenter might hear the shots if he had lost his way, but just as I was beginning to get really worried, he returned. He had followed a trail leading west from Bejucal to an aguada about three leagues off.

In late afternoon Lafleur returned with most heartening news. They had found the ruins and three stelae, two of which were sculptured and one which was plain. For a while he said it looked as though José would collapse, but he nursed the boy along. It was very encouraging news to all and put spirits into everyone.

That night, probably because he had overdone at my insistence, José had a hot fever and was delirious. I felt responsible. He groaned and cried and felt sure he was going to die in the bush. Lafleur worked over him with hot compresses and morphine. By 10:00 he was quiet, after which the doctor retired.

May 5, Friday

A remarkable day, all things considered. About 8:00 we left for the ruins. An hour and a half in a southerly direction brought us to the champas of San Leandro, where we left our horses and proceeded the rest of the way on foot.

We filled our canvas buckets at the aguada and started off in a westerly direction, Alfonso in the lead. He lost the picado once or twice but in a half hour we were skirting the right hand edge of a small ravine, on the edge of which the ruin stands.

José was truthful enough. He had seen a stela with a figure on it. The figure was in an excellent state of preservation, but oh, what a bitter disappointment after all these weary leagues. The glyphs, the only three on the front, were almost entirely effaced, and those on the sides so far gone as to be almost doubtful.

The stela next to this was broken off, and the top missing. The figure was so badly weathered that I could find no glyphs at all. I was downcast because it looked as though all our efforts had been for naught. Lafleur showed me the plain stela, a good example of its kind, but what was such to offer to one starving for dates. In the meantime Carpenter had disappeared, but a shout soon advised that he had found something. "Here are some glyphs." The cry brought me to his side quickly. To my great delight, I found he had discovered a stela with an Initial Series on one side. Although somewhat effaced, I could read its date very clearly as 9.16.0.0.0 2*Ahau*

13 *Tzec* [A.D. 751]. Black disappointment instantly gave way to complete satisfaction. All those weary leagues, those heated arguments, those "multitudinous humbugs" had not been in vain.

Between the plain stela and the one Carpenter had found was another large stone which apparently had fallen face up. While I was deciphering the date on the second stela, Carpenter had continued around the sides of this plaza where he found several more stones. Three of these appeared to be altars and the fourth, a broken stela. The latter had glyphs on its sides but it is in very bad condition. The altar in front of this stela was six feet in diameter and had nine plain circles on top around the edge. Again Carpenter disappeared and again a shout, this time from both Alfonso and Carpenter. They had discovered another stela bearing glyphs. I turned toward their shouts.

The new find was a large monument with an Initial Series on one side. Its katun [approximately twenty year period] coefficient is surely 1, 2. or 3; its tuns [approximately one year period] 11, 12, or 13; its uinals [Maya month of twenty days] and kins [Maya day] 0, and the day 2 *Ahau* and the month 13? I had not brought the tables [Goodman chronological tables] with me and did not have time to work this out in my head. When I returned to camp, however, I found it was 9.3.13.0.0 2*Ahau* 13 *Ceh* [A.D. 507].

Here was ample recompense—two dated stelae, one of them the third oldest monument heretofore reported. It was a splendid find.

We looked around for other monuments, but barring two plain ones that Carpenter found, nothing more was encountered. As we were planning to return to the champas to eat lunch, Alfonso came in with a wonderful story. He had cruised around in the bush and had found another ruin group. A house, high and complete, five stones, two carved standing stones, one fifteen feet high with a double row of letters on its back. We hurried back to the champas to eat a lunch of tea, sardines, crackers, and fruit. How good it tasted with the magic sauce of anticipation.

Without wasting much time over the repast however, we sallied forth in the same direction as in the morning. Only now we climbed the left bank of the same little ravine. Skirting along the edge of this, we soon came to the big house. We climbed up into it and found it in fairly good condition, though the front had fallen in. As it was getting late, we did not tarry long but scattered to look for the stelae. I followed Alfonso, but Carpenter had found one of the sculptured stela first.

This had an Initial Series, each glyph thereof being presented in a circular cartouche. I was unable to decipher it off hand, but it is either in Katun 6 or Katun 7, 8, or 9.

A shout from Alfonso, albeit a faint one, summoned us to another stela, his fifteen footer. This is a stone nine and a half feet above ground by actual measurement, and now leaning some two to three feet out of the perpendicular. The front tips forward and has a human figure carved on it. The sides are plain.

The back of this leaning stela makes it the most important monument in the Maya area, for it undoubtedly presents a Cycle 8 Initial Series [Stela 9, for forty-five years the oldest dated Maya stela and now known to be some thirty-six years younger than one found at Tikal within the last decade]. Careful examination of the cycle coefficient established that it could only be 8. The katun coefficient is surely above 10 and under 16, the tun 5 or 10; the uinal 11, 12, or 13; the kin 15 or 16; the day over 5 and under 11. It was getting too late to linger, but I feel sure that I will be able to decipher this when I come to examine it closely. After seeing one or two more plain stelae, we returned to the champas, saddled our horses, and rode two leagues to Bejucal. By pushing our mounts, we got in by half past 5:00, thoroughly tired but well satisfied with the day's work. Poor Alfonso found that no one had cut his ramoneo until 3:00 and in consequence ten of our seventeen mules had strayed.

May 6, Saturday

It seemed best to move our camp to San Leandro, inasmuch as there is water there and it is so much nearer the ruins. I took this up with Alfonso, and he said if he could find his missing ten mules before 11:00, he would come over. Lafleur, Andrew, and I went to the ruins. We pushed our animals and made it in an hour and fifteen minutes. We found the flies so bad at the champas that we decided to take the horses on to the ruins, hoping the flies would not be so annoying there. This proved useless, however, and the horses were soon covered with blood. Andrew's mule became so beside himself that he chewed the rope in order to free himself.

The first thing I did was to get Lafleur and Andrew to cut the line of sight around the Great Plaza [Group A]. I set to work drawing the inscription on the south side of Stela 2, the one with the Katun 16 Initial Series. I finished this before noon and made some headway on the survey of the Great Plaza before lunch.

After lunch we returned to the ruins to work at Group A. We opened up the lines of sight on the north, west, and south sides of the Great Plaza and commenced the survey in these places. We returned to Bejucal between 5:00 and 6:00, tired but satisfied. One mule was still missing, and Alfonso did not seem inclined to move camp. As I insisted, he finally consented to move us tomorrow.

May 7, Sunday

In order that camp should surely be moved, I left Andrew behind to get things under way and took Juan with me in his place. Lafleur and I set out first. I began to draw Stela 3, the early monument which I found out by my calculations to be 9.3.13.0.0   2 *Ahau* 13 *Ceh*. This job held me all the rest of the morning. About 11:00 Carpenter and Marius showed up with a long tale of woe. Carpenter thought we might be on the verge of a general mutiny, in the course of which we would be left to pilot ourselves and our impedimenta back to El Cayo. Marius also had tales of grumbling and insubordination, and altogether they were very gloomy. I did not take much stock in the idea that we would be abandoned outright, or at all, but the gloom persisted. When we reached the champas, we found our mulada had arrived.

After lunch Marius and I came back to the ruins. I drew Stela 1 and made the final measurements for the map of the Great Plaza of Group A. While doing the latter, I lost my last ruler and fear I will be greatly handicapped when it comes to drawing the monuments at Group B. Lafleur did not come out to the ruins this afternoon and thereby escaped a good drenching.

When we got back to camp, Carpenter was out scouting through the bush. He came in just before dinner to report a new group, Group C [now called Group D] with at least one new sculptured stela, intaglio carving, and several plain stelae. He describes the sculptured monument as being of a very archaic appearance. After supper, we looked for the north star and found it twinkling through a mass of foliage. Carpenter thinks he will be able to make his observations on it all right.

May 8, Monday

Shortly after we got up, Chon came to camp with an occelated turkey and a kambul. The former was indeed a perfect specimen, and it promised delectable eating. If I dwell on eating so much it is not because we are gourmets but because our fare is really getting pitifully slender. Carpenter and Lafleur skinned the turkey before we left for the ruins.

The plan this morning was to raise the Katun 3 stela which seemed as though it might have fallen face downward. All except José assembled for the turning, nine men in all. We got the stone, which weighs approximately two tons, up on one edge, until it must have been fifty degrees with the ground, enough to see that it had a sculptured face. The figure there presented is in excellent condition. I made out the head of the god which stands for the number 7. I have passed over the work which raising this monolith entailed. But my silence should not be taken as indicating that no labor was expended. The sweat, the curses, the directions in Spanish and English, the straining of muscles and tempers to the point of exhaustion, were enough if applied at one time to have moved the pyramid of Cheops. Even then we failed to get it upright. It became apparent finally that we were too exhausted to work efficiently, so we called it off for a final try tomorrow.

My "drawing hand" was ruined for the morning, so Carpenter, Lafleur, Marius, and I went to see his new site which lies about a half mile east or northeast of the champas. There are two sculptured stelae and six plains. I saw all except two of the latter. One of the sculptured stela had two columns of intaglio relief carved on the back. Unfortunately, the detail is quite gone; I was unable to decipher a single glyph. After making a sketch map of the plaza where these monuments were located, we returned to the champas for lunch.

May 9, Tuesday

Got my cuadrilla of hearties together early for the attempt on the half-turned stela. We tried a new plan, namely to tie a strong pole to the monument and another smaller one on the other side so the first would not flip, and then by pulling with a rope and raising with a pole at the same time, we hoped to lift it upright. This plan was the last shot in our quiver. If it failed, I knew we would have to abandon the attempt. It was an anxious moment, therefore, when we finally got the rope and poles adjusted and began to pull. Slowly the heavy stone swung upright. As our strength was exhausted, we rested while the rope held what we had gained. Thus, little by little, we pulled the stela erect.

There are no glyphs on the front, but the relief is in good condition. The figure holds the ceremonial bar horizontal across his breast. The left hand head appears to be that of the sun god. After getting the stone upright, we disbanded, Andrew, Chon, Alfonso, and Galileo returning to camp, Carpenter and Marius remaining to clean and photograph the stone.

Lafleur, Juan, and I went to Site B to begin my work there. While I was drawing the stela with the glyphs in single cartouches, Lafleur went to see the tall leaning stela. During the course of a two hour absence he managed to lose himself, find Carpenter, lose himself again, and bring up at the ramonal, find the workers there, return to camp and then to Group B. I had finished drawing three glyphs. It was after noon, so we returned to camp for lunch. Later I returned to finish the three glyphs on the other side of the same stela.

I finished this monument about 3:00, and then called to Lafleur who was supposed to be making a trail from it to the leaning monument. In answer to his shouts, Juan and I set off on his highway. This was astonishingly clear at first, but soon it petered to a picado which we lost. Finally, by following Lafleur's voice through the bush, we reached him, but to his great amazement, from the opposite direction from that by which his trail entered.

I was mucking around the ruck of plain stelae in front of the principal mound on this second plaza when I noticed a small fragment with glyphs on it stuck edgewise in the earth. A little search in the immediate vicinity showed what appeared to be the top of a stela. This was broken into several fragments, but on turning it over, it proved to have fallen face down and presented an exquisite example of Maya art. The carving was of the very highest order, the material a fine grained yellow limestone, and all together I think it must have been the equal of the beautiful Stela 32 at Naranjo. Fortunately, the inscription on the left side was well preserved and unmistakably recorded the date 9.19.0.0.0 9*Ahau* 10 *Mol* [A.D. 810]. I commenced drawing the Initial Series and finished all but the tun and uinal glyphs. By searching the platform above I found the base of the monument and the round altar associated with it. Digging here, I unearthed a few more fragments with glyphs. Also below in the plaza level I found another large fragment, apparently presenting the waist and breast of the figure.

Reached camp after 6:00, highly elated with this latest discovery. We will leave tomorrow. They will break camp early in the morning and we will follow them over to Bejucal in the late afternoon.

May 10, Wednesday

We were all up early. Juan got his draft and set off before dawn. For the first time since he showed Lafleur the way to the ruins, a week ago tomorrow, José worked. There seemed to be no help for it. Juan had gone, and Andrew had to see to the moving of the camp. Alfonso, Galileo, and Chon, of course, had to stay by the mulada. Marius had to aid Carpenter. Therefore, José, Lafleur, and I went to Group B by ourselves. I finished drawing the Initial Series on the beautiful stela found yesterday. After completing this, I began to copy the leaning stela. I have already touched upon this important inscription, which presents the earliest date yet deciphered. This date I was unable to decipher the first day I saw this monument, but a careful examination by standing on a scaffold which Lafleur and José had built against the stone established the original reading to have been 8.14.10.13.15 8*Men* 8 *Kayab*. In the correlation of Maya and Christian chronologies which I am advocating, this corresponds to A.D. 50 [later changed to A.D. 328].The style of the monument is sufficiently archaic to warrant this date. The glyph blocks are irregular in outline and archaic in form. It was difficult to draw because of this irregularity. It was nearly 1:00 when I finished.

Lafleur and I set off for the ruins again a little after 2:00. At the fork of the trail I left him to go on to B, while I went back to A for a few minutes to see the big stela we turned. Arthur Carpenter had cleaned it up, but in some places the relief, which is low, is badly weathered. Unfortunately, one of the places which has suffered most has been the head and face. I took final notes on the intaglio Initial Series of Stela 5, and then went back to the fork and trail to B.

As I climbed the ravine, I heard monkeys roaring in the tree tops. This noise increased in violence as I approached the Great Plaza of Group B, and just as I entered the court, it reached its climax in a final roar followed by a heavy thud. I felt Lafleur had at last landed his heart's desire, a big baboon. This was exactly the case. He and José between them had brought down a big black male monkey. They hit it four times, and even in spite of the sixty foot fall, there seemed to be a last spark of life in the poor creature after it reached the ground. It was literally alive with beef worms and smelled unto high heaven. Lafleur decided to take all parts of it not subject to immediate putrefaction to El Cayo. But for the present, we had other things to do.

Carpenter and Marius left for camp and Group A while Lafleur and I set to work taking the necessary notes for a sketch map of the plaza of Group B, sufficient to locate the monuments. This took us until 5:00. A rain was coming on, and a good mile separated us from the champas. Lafleur strung the monkey on a pole and, carrying this on our shoulders, we set out, the monkey, an ugly hairy blob, bobbing between us.

We set off for camp at a good rate as the rain was rapidly approaching. It had suddenly grown quite dark, and our time was limited. As we came out of the ravine, we struck a more rapid pace, and when the rain finally caught us, a short distance from the champas, we were fairly running through the bush with our ugly burden lurching between us. Carpenter and Marius were already at the hut, the rain was coming down in torrents. After it cleared, Carpenter had to take a few final photographs. By this time, the animals were all saddled for a two hour ride, the last half hour of which was in pitch darkness.

Several mishaps occurred then. Lafleur's horse stumbled, turned a sommersault and fell, the doctor himself clearing the plunging animal by a happy jump. My beast went to his knees but made a quick recovery. Marius's mule shied, and by a sideways jump unseated Marius, who came to Mother Earth promptly. Carpenter contracted an escoba spine in his belly in an unsuccessful encounter with a tree of that family. The greatest danger was from the horses' stepping on and being pierced by sharp sticks or from our being hit on our heads by low trees and bejucos. I was glad to see the lights of camp and hear the voices of the boys. This is the second time I have been caught in the bush after dark, and I do not like it.

Andrew had a good dinner ready for us, and against the hard day ahead, we all turned in early.

May 11, Thursday

Now that the time has finally come for starting out, preparations for leaving went forward speedily. No mules were missing. The loading was not too lengthily protracted, and at 5:25 we bid farewell to Bejucal. We had not been going long before an uproar ahead told of something up. It seems that a deer had darted under Alfonso's mule, and then made off into the bush. Our valiant hunters tried to get a shot but did not succeed.

In an hour and a half we came to the fork which caused all our trouble a week ago yesterday. Twenty minutes later we passed the champas on the north side of the bajo. The bajo itself had grown no shorter during the last week, and it took us just the same length of time to cross it that it did in going. We reached Las Positas at 1:10, four and three-quarters hours on the road. I made a lunch of Horlick's malted milk. The aguada here is fairly good and the champas excellent.

I spent the afternoon in map making, Lafleur in cooking his monkey, and Carpenter in hunting. Supper was saltless but consisted of a good kambul.

May 12, Friday

Everyone was up on time but when the mules came in, three were missing. Then commenced a long hunt until 9:00, when all were rounded up. Alfonso and Chon had a scrap and the former fired the latter, so he started off on foot for San Clemente, carrying his pack. José started next. Then Carpenter and Marius, and lastly Lafleur and I, together with Andrew, Alfonso, and Galileo, got off with the mulada. The mules went very slowly, and what we did coming in to the bush in over three hours, took us more than four coming out. Just before we reached Esperanza we met the Paredes mulada going into the bush. They are bringing out chicle and are now at Triumfo. The boy in charge told us very disquieting news.

It seems that the revolutionaries are still at Laguna and have killed a man. It was discouraging to hear this and makes us wish we could push on at once to Triumfo, where we felt more accurate information was to be had. The last league dragged very slowly and it was just 2:00 when we reached San Clemente. Here a piece of unsuspected good luck awaited us. José had killed a mule deer. In anticipation of the feast ahead of us, everyone's spirits rose.

But while we were eating our venison steak, Alfonso and Galileo reported that twelve of our fourteen mules had escaped to the bush just as they were approaching the ramonal. Furthermore, a large tamagus, two meters long, coiled in the roots of a sapote tree, had very nearly struck Galileo. Alfonso shot him. He said the sight so unnerved him that he was trembling like a leaf. Indeed he had killed another shorter snake before he returned. He said he valued his life more than a bunch of mules and would not go into the bush at night for any mulada. All we can hope now is that they will not stray far.

May 13, Saturday

I got Alfonso up at 3:00 and he went out looking for the mules. About 6:00 he returned with twelve animals, more than I thought possible. The missing ones were those ridden by Lafleur, Carpenter, José, and me. After breakfast Alfonso went out again in one direction, Galileo and Marius in another. Several hours later Alfonso brought in Lafleur's and my horses and an hour later the other two. Finally at 10:25 we started, almost our latest start. Some three hours easy riding brought us to Triumfo.

Here we found five or six men burying Lafleur's syphilitic patient. The poor devil died yesterday noon, and owing to the rocky nature of the soil, they had difficulty in giving him the six feet we are all supposed to be entitled to. But the news here quickly drove thoughts of this one out of our heads.

The Salama Battalion of the Guatemalan army is reported as being at Plancha. The rebels are at Laguna. So our objective—El Cayo—lies just the other side of a line joining the two hostile camps. Our problem is how to reach Cayo safely and expeditiously. Three general routes are under consideration. First, to follow the road by which we came in until we cross the Holmul, then leave it, take to the bush on a due easterly course until we have entered the colony, which cannot be more than ten or twelve miles distant at this point, and then swing southeast until we strike the Belize River or some road leading into Cayo. I have placed this route first, since it leaves but little opportunity to our guides to double-cross us in any way. The second alternative is that favored by Alfonso and Chon, which is to ride to the Río Holmul, where we would cross it by another more westerly pass, leave the road to take a southeasterly course through the bush straight to Cayo. This has in its favor that Chon knows the bush in this vicinity, and that it is doubtless our shortest course and probably therefore the easiest. It has a serious drawback, however, in that it is by all odds the most perilous route, since it traverses the country between the two hostile camps, a country which I believe must be filled with outlooks and pickets. Even when we reach the line, we may run into the Colonial troops. The third alternative is to strike due south from the river until we cut the Flores trail and then come into Plancha from the west. Naturally, Alfonso does not want to leave his mules. As there is no one here to take care of them, it looks as though we would have to leave him behind and trust ourselves to Chon and José. Lencho Paredes, whose mulada we met yesterday, is due here tomorrow. Alfonso thinks he might get an arriero from him, in which event he would go on with us. If Lencho does not turn up tomorrow, we will go through with Chon by the middle route.

May 14, Sunday
No entry.

May 15, Monday
I was awake at 3:00 and awakened Andrew and the others at 4:00. We all got up at once, dressed, and finished what little packing we had left. By 5:30 we were all through breakfast, and then commenced the regular morning humbug of one animal missing. This time it was Carpenter's horse. One of Charley's animals also could not be found. There was a little talk of staying over another day, but I quashed this as much as I could. Fortunately, the two missing animals were found in a short time, and packing went forward rapidly. There are eighteen of us now in the two joined muladas and some thirty-odd mules.

As we left the champas and crossed the Río Triumfo, it was just 7:30. We followed our old trail back for two hours, and then missed the fork to Corozal, which lost us fifteen minutes. Just before this mishap, we passed Trinidad Flores' mulada. The usual confusion incident to these occasions ensued, and after the two muladas had disentangled themselves, each went his way.

We lost another fifteen minutes at Corozal by taking another wrong trail, but finally got started right. Fortunately the two muladas kept close together, and straying mules were promptly detected and more promptly brought back into the straight and narrow path. An hour before getting in, Lafleur's horse suddenly failed. Examination showed it had sustained a four inch cut between the forelegs. Lafleur dismounted and had to walk. Shortly afterward the road began to pass through a large group of mounds, which continued on and off for three quarters of an hour, when we reached our journey's end. We camped a little beyond the regular paraje because the water at the first aguada was so poor.

There are no champas where we stopped, but the boys say it will not rain. We are trusting to luck. After a cup of hot Horlick's malted milk, Carpenter and I returned to examine the big site through which we had come.

The ramoneros were felling their trees somewhere off to the north, and we went in this general direction, leaving the trail at the first large mound on the left. It wasn't long before Carpenter had found a large stela and in front of it a round altar. The stela had fallen face downward, and all the back had disintegrated. The sides are plain. The face we could not determine, but we are inclined to think it is plain as all the other stelae I examined here (3) are plain.

Leaving this mound and bearing off to the west we came to another mound on top of which two of Charley's boys were felling ramon. In front of this was one of the widest stela I have ever seen. It was at least six feet wide and eight or ten feet high. The top was broken off and fallen to one side. Two square altars with well rounded corners were associated with the stela. The front, back, and sides of the stela were plain.

Escaping from this vicinity just in time to miss being hit by the falling ramon trees, we continued our peregrinations. We rounded the corner of a very large mound and commenced ascending the back. About half way up, we climbed over the ruins of a double range of rooms, the inner chamber not being more than two feet wide. Continuing on up over these we still had a stiff climb before we reached the summit of the mound. From here through the thick foliage on the sides we caught glimpses of large stretches of country on all sides. We saw we were on the summit of a low ridge extending roughly east and west.

An exclamation from the lynx-eyed Carpenter attracted me. "I see a whale of a ruin to the west." Sure enough, there pricked out against the western horizon on top of a distant ridge was a large city, with its main pyramid, a lofty structure, surmounted by a high temple with its roof-comb. To the left and right stretched a long chain of minor mounds and constructions, the whole being a half a mile long as presented to us. The sight of it took my breath away, held me spellbound. What could it be? Surely no city of such size could have remained undiscovered in this region. It appeared to be between ten to fifteen miles west of us. My mind flashed to Tikal. But at

Tikal are five tall pyramid temples. Then I knew it must be Nakum. The position was about right for Nakum, and the one pyramid temple suited it to a T. We ardently wished we had brought the binoculars so we could see the city better. This wish grew so strong that Carpenter finally decided to return to camp for them. I was to remain behind on the top to guide him by my shouts back to the temple.

He was not gone too long, though the flies, mosquitos, and other insects in that lofty place had well-nigh devoured me before he finally got back. The binoculars swept away the cobwebs of the intervening miles and brought the city almost to our very feet. It towered there above that distant ridge, silhouetted against the roseate glow of the late afternoon light, a thing of towers, pyramids, turrets, and minarets.

May 16, Tuesday

We actually were under way today by 6:40. Our interest, since the rebels are supposedly not to be encountered until tomorrow, centered in whether we would be able to get Bradley's wounded horse through to El Cayo. It is badly puffed with air, but the cut itself, though open, remains sweet and wholesome owing to that wonderful cure-all of Dr. Underhill's [physician on earlier Carnegie Expedition that season]. Of course, he was very stiff, and did not want to make the start, but after he had been on the way for a league, he was sufficiently limbered up to dart into the bush, tangle himself up and pause to eat *sapotes*. Our anxiety over him gradually decreased, and the seven long hot hours between Dos Aguadas and the river claimed our unwilling attention.

The trail for the first two hours led south, then worked around gradually to the east and was actually making north when we reached the river at 1:30. About two hours before getting there, we passed some champas from which a right hand trail led off to Laguna Colorado. I passed through this latter place when I went to Nakum last year. We finished the last of the malted milk for lunch, and then fell to on Bradley's animal. Lafleur and Carpenter gave it a massage, pricking the skin at intervals to let out the air. They also applied the Underhill medicine. Although stiff, the horse stood the journey well. I did not send him to the ramonal but got some corn from Charley. This so heartened him that he tried to make off about 9:00 and had to be tied for the night. Lafleur put the finishing touches on the cooking of his monkey before night drew in, and against what may be an exciting day tomorrow, we opened our last tin of milk, one Carpenter had secreted against this fateful day. Chon came in late as usual but with no game. The camp was picturesque in the moonlight. The moon is almost full and shed a radiance which quite dimmed our electric lamps and the kerosene lanterns.

May 17, 18 and 19

It is with a heavy heart that I take up the closing pages of this diary, whose ending has been so unexpectedly tragic with the death of Lafleur. The entries for May 17, 18, and 19 were never written. Instead, five days later at El Cayo, I wrote the first half of my official report of the tragedy to Dr. R.S. Woodward, President of the Institution, tracing the series of events which had led up to it, from the day we left El Cayo for the interior, April 25th, down to the morning of May 17th, the day of Dr. Lafleur's death.

On May 31st, at Belize, I wrote the second half of this report, covering the events from the morning of May 17th down to June 2nd, the day we left El Cayo for Belize.

This report, in the form of these two letters to the President of the Institution, has been included here as the closing part of my diary for 1916.

El Cayo, British Honduras
May 22, 1916

My dear Dr. Woodward:

On May 19th, as soon as I could gather and verify the essential facts, I advised you by wireless of the death of Dr. Moise Lafleur, the expedition's physician, which occurred two days earlier (May 17) at three o'clock in the afternoon. The more detailed account which follows has been prepared after repeated consultations with Mr. Carpenter, and the two colored boys, Andrew and Marius Silas, the only other eye-witnesses of the tragedy beside myself.

In order that you may understand clearly just what happened, it is first necessary for me to outline the movements of the expedition during the past four weeks, and to describe briefly, not only the geography of the country in which it had been operating, but also the attendant political circumstances.

The expedition left Belize on the 17th of April, five strong, Mr. Carpenter, Dr. Lafleur, myself, and our two colored servants, Andrew and Marius Silas. We reached here (El Cayo), the head of navigation on the Belize River, three days later; and at once began to arrange for a three weeks trip into northern Petén, the adjoining department of the Republic of Guatemala.

Having gathered the necessary outfit, guides, mules, supplies, etc., we left El Cayo on April 25th, taking a generally northwesterly direction into the Petén bush, our objective being a newly reported archaeological site five days journey in.

The northern half of Petén is a gently rolling plain traversed by ranges of low hills, and is completely overgrown with a vast tropical jungle. The only roads are narrow winding trails cut by chicleros (i.e., the chicle bleeders), and the only human habitations in the region, their constantly shifting camps. You should note that these trails spread fanlike from El Cayo as a base. Here all the mule trains discharge their cargoes, and from here the chicle is shipped to Belize by water. To the west and north lies a vast trackless jungle whose only point of egress is at this village of El Cayo.

Along one of the blades of this fan of trails we were now making our way. The first night out (Ojo de Agua) one of our guides to whom I had advanced money after the custom of the country, decamped, presumably returning to El Cayo. The next morning (April 26th) I went back to look for him, leaving Mr. Carpenter in charge with the understanding that he was to proceed to Laguna with the rest of the party that same day and await me there.

On reaching El Cayo I heard some startling news. That very morning at daybreak, a party of about forty revolutionists, composed mostly of Mexican chicleros actually recruited on British soil, i.e., from El Cayo and Benque Viejo, had captured the frontier village of Plancha Piedra without bloodshed, and had seized the chicle and mule trains there. They were issuing manifestos to the effect that nobody would be harmed, and that their movement was directed solely against the Government of Guatemala, and the really infamous abuses which have crept into the chicle business here.

I felt that I must return at once to Laguna, and acquaint the other members of the party with this totally unexpected development, and by a long ride I succeeded in reaching there after dark that same night.

We considered the situation carefully, debating whether to continue on our way, or whether to return to El Cayo at once. Because it was impossible to foresee all the contingencies which might arise if we went on, I did not care to assume entire responsibility for the decision, and the question was left to an open vote of the field staff: Mr. Carpenter, Dr. Lafleur, and myself. We found ourselves unanimous as to the advisability of continuing our journey, which opinion, indeed, was held by all the others, the native guides, muleteers, and camp servants; and I may add here, that in so far as the little band of revolutionaries, which captured Plancha Piedra on April 26th, was concerned, it was in no way responsible for the doctor's murder, a matter solely chargeable to the Guatemalan troops. The next morning therefore (April 27th) we continued our journey into the bush, turning our backs upon civilization, and largely forgetting the matter for the next fortnight.

This is not the proper time for presenting the scientific results of this trip, probably the most successful I have ever undertaken, since it includes among other things, the discovery of the oldest Maya monument yet reported; so I will pass over the intervening fortnight between April 29th and May 13th, without further comment other than to say that we made the journey successfully; spent six days at the ruins [Uaxactún] near a chicle camp called San Leandro; and returned, back along our trail, reaching the chicle camp of Triumfo on May 15th, where we heard the first accurate news in two weeks of the conditions obtaining ahead of us.

We learned that the revolutionists had abandoned Plancha Piedra almost immediately after they had taken it, and marching to Laguna, had taken that village without opposition on the 28th of April, the day after we left there. The Government troops in the meantime had reoccupied Plancha Piedra, and had fortified themselves there. In these two places the respective forces were encamped, apparently watching each other.

The only weak point about this news was its age, being then (May 13th) over two weeks old. We did not know, nor had we any means of finding out, what had happened since. The entire trouble might have blown over in that time, or might equally as well have reached serious proportions. In this dilemma we decided to wait over for a day at Triumfo, particularly since another mule train, whose advance runners we had met the previous day, was due to arrive the next day, and its leader, so my own head muleteer told me, knew more about the situation ahead of us than we did since he had left El Cayo after us.

The next day (May 14th) this mule train arrived, and with it began the first of those adverse circumstances which in a vicious train so linked themselves together as to eventuate in Dr. Lafleur's death.

There arrived that same day at Truimfo another mule train also enroute for El Cayo. With it came a Mexican named Ladislao Romero, a chicle contractor, and for the last seven years a resident of El Cayo. He had been sent into the bush from El Cayo by a Mr. Waight, another chicle contractor, a British subject, for the purpose of hiding Waight's chicle in the bush until the trouble should have passed over. He carried a passport from the Commissioner of the Cayo District, the local colonial administrative official; and to provide against possible encounters with the revolutionists, he had gone first to Laguna and had secured from their chief, one Trinidad Flores, a passport permitting him and his associates to pass freely through the revolutionary lines.

Romero approached me at Triumfo that afternoon (May 14th) and told me that a mutual friend, no less than the revolutionary chief himself, whom I had known slightly at El Cayo, sent me his best wishes and the message that if I cared to return to El Cayo through Laguna I would not be molested in any way. He then showed me a passport signed by this Trinidad Flores, which in fact gave him and his associates free passage through the revolutionary lines. At the same time he also showed me another passport from the District Commissioner of the Cayo District giving him permission to leave and return to the Colony for the business in hand. Romero said the only thing he lacked was a passport from the Guatemalan authorities. Of the latter I had taken elaborate precautions to provide myself with what I thought was an adequate supply for any emergency that might arise. Both Mr. Carpenter and I had letters from the Minister of Foreign Relations in Guatemala City bespeaking for us the usual courtesies extended to scientific expeditions, and in addition I had a letter from Don Clodeveo Berges, the Governor of Petén, recommending me to the care of all the civil and military authorities of the Department. Finally, besides these we had our own American passports and your official letter, sufficient credentials, if examined, to guarantee the peaceful and altruistic character of our mission.

By traveling with Romero we would be safe if we encountered any of the revolutionists, and so far as any government troops were concerned, we naturally anticipated no danger from that source. Moreover, by joining forces with this other mule train we increased our number from 9 to 18, a greater number than any picket of the revolutionists which we would be likely to encounter.

We left Triumfo the next morning (May 15th) and proceeding by more circuitous and less used trails than the ones by which we had entered, we reached Dos Aguadas that evening and the Río Holmul the next (May 16th). By this route we made a big detour to the south and west in order to avoid the revolutionary headquarters at Laguna. We had at last reached the region where trouble—if there were to be any—would most likely occur. You will note that from the Río Holmul to El Cayo is only a matter of thirty miles, and from this point the trails converge more or less rapidly. This last stretch lay directly between the two hostile camps, and we imagined must be fairly well patrolled by both sides. Unfortunately there were no other trails available since, as I have already explained, all trails emerge at El Cayo; and we had no guides who could lead us through the untracked bush, even had our failing food supply permitted such a course. No one, not even the natives, expected any serious trouble since we had passports from both sides, and indeed the worst we ourselves anticipated was that we might be stopped, and some of our outfit taken from us.

I now come to the last day (May 17th), that on which Dr. Lafleur was killed. We left the Río Holmul at 7:50, our party going out in two sections, one taking the pack animals over the Bullet Tree Falls trail, and the other in which Mr. Carpenter, Dr. Lafleur, and I all rode, going by way of Chunvis.

We approached this latter place with an extreme of caution. The bell had been removed from the bell-mare; no one spoke aloud; all shouting at the mules, the inevitable accompaniment of mule driving in this country, was eliminated for once; and our really large mule train made little or no noise. When within two miles of Chunvis three runners were sent ahead to find out whether or not the coast was clear. By missing the trail at this point we also missed the boy they sent back to inform us that all was safe and to come ahead in, but this was of little consequence since we ourselves reached Chunvis a little later finding everything there perfectly quiet and normal.

The two chicleros in charge of the camp told us that the government troops were still at Plancha Piedra from which they had not moved since they occupied it three weeks before; and that the revolutionists were still at Laguna from which they had not moved since they captured it. Furthermore that there had been no encounter between the two forces, and that all was, and had been, quiet. Indeed, a mule train had been engaged for the past week in making a daily round-trip from Buena Vista in the Colony to Chunvis and return for chicle, and finally this train had left for Buena Vista three hours before we got in.

This then was the information we received at Chunvis, and it dispelled all our misgivings. Everything was, and had been, quiet since the original outbreak more than three weeks before, the regular business of hauling out chicle was going on uninterruptedly as always, and indeed over the very trail we were about to take to El Cayo.

The day was early, just noon; the horses while not fresh, were by no means exhausted; and the remaining distance not more than eighteen miles. We were unanimous in the decision to push through to El Cayo, get our mail, and the first news of the outside world in over three weeks. Back of this decision also, was the feeling that a short ten miles separated us from the frontier, and once across this line and on British soil, we could dismiss all further anxiety over the revolutionists.

But here a quandary arose. The head muleteer of the pack train said his pack animals were too tired to go on, and he was not coming in until the next day. This left us without a guide. I asked some of the chicleros if they would show us the trail to Buena Vista, but they could not leave their chicle. Finally Romero said he would go with us as far as Buena Vista, from which point on in to El Cayo I myself knew the trail. I closed the arrangements with him, and at 12:40 P.M. we started six strong: Romero, Mr. Carpenter, Dr. Lafleur, Andrew and Marius Silas, and myself, all mounted. Andrew Silas led, in addition, a horse which had been hurt on the way.

The guide Romero rode first, I came second after my usual custom. The other four constantly shifted their positions in the line behind us. The country between Chunvis and the border is a succession of low hills covered with the same dense bush as elsewhere. The trail bears a little south of east and as it approaches the frontier, it ascends a low hill cutting across the slope—in the direction we were going—from right to left.

Just a few minutes before the murder, perhaps fifteen at the outside, occurred an incident which had an important bearing on the matter, since it probably determined (without our knowing it) that Dr. Lafleur was to lose his life instead of myself.

About 2:30 a sudden brief shower came up. The water collecting on the lenses of my glasses so interfered with my vision that I took them off to place in my pocket until the rain should be over. In so doing they fell to the ground, and I was obliged to dismount to pick them up. At this point Dr. Lafleur, who had been riding well toward the rear, pushed up ahead of me saying as he passed, "I'm going up next to the guide, Morley, to talk to him." Andrew Silas leading the lame horse also passed me before I remounted and fell into line.

This trivial incident, you will note, caused an entire shifting in our relative positions in the line. Romero, the guide, was still first, but Dr. Lafleur had taken my place as second, and Andrew Silas and the lame animal had come forward to the third place, I then fell back to the fourth place, Mr. Carpenter came fifth, and Marius Silas last. This could not have been more than five minutes before the shooting.

We proceeded noisily enough through the bush, with no thought of concealing our presence there, talking back and forth to one another, all fears at rest. The frontier was within a quarter of a mile. I had told Romero to advise me in advance when we approached the line so that we could take the readings of our watches since we were carrying out observations for longitude. He had just called back to me that we were getting very near the line. We had entered a space about one hundred twenty-five feet long where the underbrush had been cleared back from the trail some distance on the left hand side and a few yards on the right hand side leaving us in a little clearing. Ahead the thick undergrowth closed in again.

Suddenly without warning of any kind, not the stirring of a leaf, there burst from the bush just ahead of us and to the right and left as well, a volley of ten or fifteen rifle shots, and this was immediately succeeded by sustained irregular firing.

Simultaneously with this first volley the guide Romero gave a violent cry, at the same time falling to the ground where he lay crying and writhing about apparently mortally wounded.

Doctor Lafleur after the first volley jumped from his horse, and paused to pump a shell from the magazine into the chamber of his gun, a Winchester 38 calibre carbine, which he was in the habit of keeping at hand while traveling for hunting purposes. An instant later he sought cover to the right of the trail. It is doubtful in the minds of Mr. Carpenter and myself whether he ever succeeded in firing a shot; particularly since the autopsy seems to show that his right arm was almost immediately disabled.

The boy Andrew, who occupied the third place in line, dismounted with maximum celerity, abandoning his own mount and the lame horse he had been leading, and retired to the rear post-haste, back down the trail toward Chunvis.

During these few seconds I retired a few feet—still mounted—until I was abreast Mr. Carpenter who had just dismounted. By this time none of the party remained between us and the firing line, which was not more than twenty-five yards distant at the maximum, and probably nearer half that. We stood here engaged in conversation between thirty-five and sixty seconds, the open target of uninterrupted fire from the ambuscade. I said, "What are they doing?" Mr. Carpenter replied, "They are shooting at us." I returned the question, "What had we better do?" He answered, "I am going to shoot." At this point the boy Marius, who had not moved from the beginning, broke in by saying, "Mr. Morley, I only have four cartridges, we'd better go back," Mr. Carpenter had, in this interval, drawn his pistol, released his horse which dashed forward through the ambuscade, and had fired twice. Up to this moment none of us had seen any member of the ambuscade, though we assumed from the first that it was the revolutionists.

Mr. Carpenter believes that as his horse passed through the ambuscade, he saw one man reaching for it, at whom he fired the two shots mentioned.

That he did see a man at this time is not entirely certain however, since the head of the clearing was already filled with powder haze.

At this point I began to realize the extreme peril of our open position, and called first to Mr. Carpenter, "Arthur, we must get back," and then gave the general command, "Back! Back! Back! For God's sake, everybody back!" I spurred my horse, wheeled and dashed down the trail around the first bend followed closely by Marius and at a greater distance by Mr. Carpenter, both on foot. Here we paused an instant and then set off at a run overtaking the boy Andrew about one hundred fifty yards from the first bend. At two hundred yards we came to the bottom of the slope and stopped.

A hurried consultation was held. Mr. Carpenter decided against my wishes, since I believed that Dr. Lafleur was dead, to approach as near as possible through the bush with the object of ascertaining whether Dr. Lafleur had survived the opening fire, and if so, to carry him cartridges which he lacked. I instructed him to return to Chunvis within the hour to which he refused to agree. He started back toward the shooting, which had practically subsided, carrying his pistol and some cartridges but leaving everything else. I started for Chunvis with the two servants. We had scarcely gone a hundred paces when two rifle shots were heard in the direction Mr. Carpenter had taken. I said, "They've got Carpenter or that is the end of the poor doctor," whereupon we quickened our pace fearing pursuit. Subsequently the servants say they heard faint shots, but I did not. Two hours later we were in Chunvis.

Morley's second letter to Dr. Woodward was written on May 31st from Belize and in part reads,

Dr. Lafleur was killed, so far as I can make out from our watches, at three o'clock in the afternoon. Two hours later we reached Chunvis and spread the alarm. The muleteers were terrified as were the chicleros, each anticipating a similar fate for himself. All were unanimous, however, that instant flight was our only course, the only disagreement being as to which was the safest trail out. The two colored boys and I, firm in the conviction that we had been attacked by revolutionists, were in favor of going out by the Benque Viejo road, i.e., that which passed nearest the headquarters of the government troops at Plancha. The five muleteers and chicleros, on the other hand, were equally certain that we had been ambushed by government troops, and consequently wanted to take the Romana, or Bullet Tree Falls trail, that is to say, one as far from the government quarters at Plancha as possible. This discussion grew warm until I silenced them by saying that we could not have been ambushed by government troops, since such would have halted us and examined our credentials.

I gave this incident simply to show that we had assumed from the first that our assailants had been revolutionists or bandits, and that far from regarding the government troops as a possible source of danger, we had from the first, and constantly throughout the trip, relied upon them as a factor of safety to be depended upon under all conditions. It was no wonder then that I refused to believe the men when they said the government troops were our assailants, and I gave the order to leave by the Benque road forthwith.

We left Chunvis about five o'clock, eight strong: myself, Andrew and Marius Silas, and five muleteers and chicleros. We had already done over twenty miles of muleback riding, and ten miles of walking and running, and were pretty well tired out.

Just before dusk (at 6:50 P.M.) we heard faintly, as from a long distance off in the general direction of Buena Vista, several volleys. I could only imagine that these were for Mr. Carpenter, and that he had been tracked down and killed.

We continued our way with even greater caution. Shortly after this night came on, and we had to proceed more slowly by the light of a lantern. Half an hour later we discovered footprints in the trail, and turned aside into a corozo palm swamp to sleep for the night. The boys were afraid to follow the trail any further because of the footprints, and it was out of the question to push on through the untracked bush at night.

Our stopping place abounded in garrapatas (ticks), and sleep, though not rest, was out of the question. Toward morning a heavy rain came up and drenched everybody.

I aroused the men at 4:30 and as soon as it was light enough to see in the bush we resumed our way. The plan was to follow the trail until it approached the immediate vicinity of the frontier, then to take to the bush and cut directly through by compass bearing to Benque Viejo, perhaps three miles off. As we approached the line, we redoubled our precautions. We were not more than two miles from Plancha at this point, and although I had no fear of the government troops, the men were in terror believing as they did that this outrage had been committed by them.

We reached the line sooner than we expected, at 7:30 A.M. The first man suddenly found himself in a clearing running north and south. The line was clear. Hastily but silently we crossed into British territory. I think I have rarely experienced greater relief than when we were on the British side, and as for the men, they openly rejoiced; threw their hats in the air like boys, withdrew the shells from their shotguns, walked more noisily and talked more cheerfully, such was their confidence in the protection of the British flag.

At 8:45 we reached the Mopan River; summoned a ferryman from the other side, and in a few minutes were in Benque, all members of the expedition at last safe in British territory with the exception of Mr. Carpenter and Dr. Lafleur.

At Benque Viejo news of another conflict greeted me. At dusk the previous evening, a party of Guatemalan government troops had attacked a force of Colonial Volunteers and constables in British territory, and had killed one of the constables, leaving two of their own men dead on the field, and losing four others from wounds while they were being carried to Plancha. This fight had taken place near Buena Vista, not more than half a mile from the spot where we had been ambushed; and now for the first time, it began to appear to me that government troops had been responsible for the attack upon our party also.

At Benque Viejo, however, I could get no information about any other shooting affray—except this killing of Corporal Flowers—and I feared that both Mr. Carpenter and Dr. Lafleur had shared the same fate. As telephone service between Benque Viejo and El Cayo was interrupted, I decided to leave at once for the latter place, hoping that one or the other might possibly have come out of the bush there.

On the way over, I met some people who told me an American had escaped from the bush late the previous night, reporting that his two companions had been killed. Although my informant could give no details, I felt confident that it was Mr. Carpenter who had escaped, and further that Dr. Lafleur was dead.

I reached El Cayo before noon, and found Mr. Carpenter at the District Commissioner's; here I secured more detailed information of the doctor's death, and of Mr. Carpenter's subsequent movements.

It is now necessary to go back to the preceding day and trace Mr. Carpenter's steps from the time I left him on the trail until I met him in El Cayo.

Mr. Carpenter, acting under the belief that our flight had carried us perhaps half a mile from the ambuscade, returned at a brisk pace along the trail, intending to take to the bush when he approached within sight of the firing line. To his astonishment, however, after rounding the second bend, he found himself back in the clearing where the attack had occurred and almost at the spot from which he had started.

A few yards ahead of him, scattered in the vicinity of the bodies, were ten or twelve of our assailants, some clearly visible, others less so because of the powder haze which still hung over the head of the clearing.

He stopped, hesitating whether to run back along the trail or seek cover in the bush. During this brief pause, he observed some taking to cover; but nevertheless, two men fired at him almost instantly. These were the shots I had heard and had imagined to have killed either Dr. Lafleur or himself.

Fortunately, these both missed him, and again he sought safety in flight around the first bend. He was hotly pursued, and realizing that his pursuers would round the same bend before he could reach the next, he darted into the bush on the right, jumped a small log some twenty-five feet from the trail, and flattened himself on the ground against it. Although his cover was entirely inadequate, eleven men passed without seeing him, and continued down the trail toward the point where he had left me. By his watch it was then 2:25 P.M., which in corrected time was 3:05. In other words, just five minutes had elapsed since the first volley.

From his hiding place a considerable portion of the trail and clearing was visible. He saw Dr. Lafleur motionless on the ground perhaps fifty yards away, surrounded by other men, some ten or twelve of whom had in the meantime emerged from the cover of the ambuscade. He had also occasional glimpses of the body of Ladislao Romero, the guide. It also remained motionless. For about half an hour he remained without moving in this precarious and awkward position, during all of which time neither body stirred and he felt entirely satisfied that both were dead. Toward the end of this time he began to formulate plans for extricating himself from his perilous position.

Having heard nothing of the men who had gone down the trail, he concluded that they were continuing the pursuit toward Chunvis. He thought by firing rapidly at those in sight a number of times he might frighten them into again taking cover long enough for him to escape. He fired his pistol, a 30 calibre Luger automatic, five times in rapid succession at a partly visible group of three or four men, who with the others about, instantly took cover. These latter shots were the last heard by Andrew Silas on our way back to Chunvis.

Unfortunately, the men who had gone in pursuit of us were close at hand, and on hearing these shots they returned at full speed. When their companions saw them returning and when no more shots were fired at them, all commenced to converge on Mr. Carpenter's position. He could see them approaching, although they could not see him.

This move obviously forced his hand, and when they had approached to within twenty yards, he ran some seventy yards deeper into the bush, where he again concealed himself behind more effective cover. By this time the men had spread out into a semi-circle and were systematically stalking the bush.

His new cover proved equally insecure, and this time he ran back a long distance until all sound of pursuit had ceased. From this point he circled back through the bush, intending to strike the Buena Vista trail beyond the ambuscade and go for help. In so doing he accidentally returned to the vicinity of the main body of our assailants who were encamped very near the lines on the British side. He saw there a greater number of men than he had thought the whole party contained, and he concluded that no part of the trail would be safe.

His presence was not discovered however, and by making a big detour and keeping to the bush, he finally emerged at Calla Creek near Buena Vista, about half-past five. As he had never been in the vicinity before, he was not certain whether he was in British territory or not but presently meeting some of the Volunteers who were patrolling the river ford at Buena Vista, he was told that he was in the Colony.

His subsequent movements may be rapidly indicated. At Buena Vista he informed the officer in charge—Corporal Flowers who was subsequently killed—what had happened, and asked for a mount to El Cayo to lay the matter before the District Commissioner. This was immediately provided, as well as a constable to accompany him, and he continued his journey to El Cayo without further delay.

Corporal Flowers, acting on Mr. Carpenter's information and the story of two chicleros who had been shot at in British territory that same afternoon, selected a number of men and at once proceeded along the Chunvis trail toward the frontier.

The details of his encounter with Guatemalan troops in British territory, in which he lost his life, are fully set forth in the report of the inquest held by the Colonial authorities, and are without the province of this report.

Mr. Carpenter reached El Cayo at 7:20 P.M. and related to the District Commissioner and the officers of the Colonial troops, who were together at dinner, the events of the afternoon.

The District Commissioner at once telegraphed the Colonial Secretary in Belize for instructions, and Mr. Carpenter at the same time communicated with the nearest American official, Consul W.L. Avery at Belize, reporting the affair and requesting immediate assistance.

Communication between El Cayo and Belize was interrupted and neither of these telegrams could be sent at the time, consequently the local authorities agreed to accompany him to the border with troops.

At 8:30 P.M. Mr. Carpenter left El Cayo for the frontier with the District Commissioner, the District Medical Officer, the Superintendent of Police, and Lieutenant Currie in command of twenty-five troops. They reached Buena Vista before midnight.

Two hours were spent in engaging and dispatching two trusted bushmen to penetrate the bush as far as Chunvis. These carried duplicate notes to me advising me that they could be trusted to guide me out in safety.

At 2:00 A.M. the entire party set out for the frontier, and at daylight reached the place where Corporal Flowers had been killed. They found his body, and those of two Guatemalans, and at the same time they frightened away some six or seven Guatemalans who had evidently been left on guard over night.

As neither the Colonial troops nor the Colonial officials could cross the frontier, Mr. Carpenter crossed on his own responsibility with the hope of bringing out Dr. Lafleur's body, taking with him one of the men who had stood by Corporal Flowers when he was killed, and the brother of our head muleteer. They worked their way carefully through the bush to within some fifty yards of the place where our party had been fired upon. Here they located a number of the enemy advantageously stationed under cover on both sides of the trail.

Not wishing to precipitate another shooting affray, they withdrew cautiously to the line, abandoning for the time being all attempts to recover Dr. Lafleur's body.

After this, the whole party returned to Buena Vista, carrying Corporal Flowers's body with them. All of the officials enumerated returned with Mr. Carpenter to El Cayo, whither they arrived some fifteen minutes ahead of me as previously set forth.

After hearing Mr. Carpenter's story, I made ready to return to Benque Viejo the same afternoon in order to get in touch with the Guatemalan officials at Plancha relative to the matter of removing Dr. Lafleur's body to El Cayo.

Pablo Guerra, the Commandante of Plancha, was the highest local official and was, theoretically at least, responsible for the entire matter. On reaching Benque Viejo, I dispatched a letter to him at Plancha, stating that I wanted written permission to cross the frontier near Buena Vista for the purpose of removing the bodies of Dr. Lafleur and the guide for burial at El Cayo. I requested the presence of a Guatemalan official as a sign of good faith, and finally intimated that if the necessary permission was not speedily forthcoming I would take the matter up directly with the central authorities in Guatemala City.

Early the next morning (May 19th) I received a letter saying we were free to remove Dr. Lafleur's body but not that of the guide, whom he claimed was a revolutionist. He guaranteed further the presence of a Guatemalan official and an armed escort at the scene of the killing.

I telephoned Mr. Carpenter to have a coffin made and the grave dug. It was arranged that he was to meet me at Buena Vista with the local Colonial physician, Dr. Lewis. The officer in charge of the Colonial Volunteers, Captain Duncan Fraser, had promised an armed escort to the frontier.

Father Versavel, S.J., first went to Plancha to see Pablo Guerra, and to sign a paper promising that we would not touch the body of the guide Romero, without which the whole proceeding could not have gone forward. Thence he was to go directly to the scene of the killing accompanied by the Guatemalan troops. I was to meet him with the Colonial escort at the frontier.

This was Friday, May 19th. I reached Buena Vista before Mr. Carpenter arrived, and engaged a dugout canoe to carry the body to El Cayo.

Mr. Carpenter, accompanied by Dr. Lewis and Lieutenant Masson, in command of the escort of Volunteers, arrived just before two and we started at once for the frontier.

After crossing the river, we ascended several low hills. The line is about two miles beyond the river. Lieutenant Masson's instructions were to halt his command of about twenty-five men fifty yards from the frontier and advance no further.

Before reaching this point, we passed the point where Corporal Flowers had been shot, and besides a mule there were the bodies of two Guatemalan soldiers who had been killed on the spot. These were well within British territory, some eighty yards from the line.

After leaving the Colonial escort, Dr. Lewis, Mr. Carpenter, and I advanced under a flag of truce to the line where we were met by Father Versavel and the officer in charge of the Guatemalan troops. Guatemalan troops to the number of thirty were drawn up on either side of the trail and saluted when we passed.

Father Versavel reported that he had already seen the body and that it was in very bad condition. We proceeded about a third of a mile along the Chunvis trail and then turned off to the right (north). Some eighty yards from the trail we found the body in a little hollow whither it had evidently been removed.

This hollow, a natural hole surrounded by a bank perhaps six feet high on all sides, was an excellent hiding place, since the body could only be seen from on top of the bank surrounding it.

The body was bound to a pole, tied at the knees and neck with tough vines, for the purpose of carrying it thither. The place where he died, i.e., on the trail, was about two hundred fifty feet distant.

I need not dwell here on the condition of the body or the nature of the wounds which caused death. These matters have been adequately covered in Dr. Lewis's report, which I have already forwarded to you. I cannot refrain, however, from commenting on the wound in the throat, undoubtedly a cut from a machete, which all but severed the head from the body. Such an act of wanton brutality even though committed after death is utterly indefensible, and I earnestly trust may be made the basis for increasing the legitimate indemnity Dr. Lafleur's heirs are entitled to.

Father Versavel recited those prayers appropriate to the occasion, and then we prepared the body for its removal. I had brought a bolt of burlap and this was now wrapped round and round the body, binding it to the pole from which, owing to its condition, it seemed best not to remove it. This was next tied securely with rope, and then the whole bundle laid on a stretcher.

The chicleros I had brought from Benque Viejo carried the body out to the line aided by Guatemalan soldiers. I had a cross cut on a large tree growing out of the hollow where the body was found, and on it wrote, "Here was found the body of Moise Lafleur, 19th of May, 1916, who died fighting bravely, May 17th, 1916."

The sergeant in command of the Guatemalan troops ordered a rough cross made, and this was put up over the spot where we had found the body.

Before leaving, I went to look at the body of the guide. It was further in the bush and had been thrown behind a log; apparently it had not been mutilated.

The Guatemalan troops were drawn up in a double line on one side of the boundary and the Colonial troops on the other. As the body passed between these lines, both commands were brought to "present arms" and held there until the body passed beyond. I stayed behind a few minutes to find out who had been in command of the troops when they attacked us the day before, but could get little accurate information. The sergeant said it had been a Captain Casasola, who had been killed in the fight with the Volunteers. I was later told that he was still living.

It was four o'clock before the body reached the river. It was very heavy, and we had to change the carriers constantly. The trail was overgrown here and there, and progress was slow. Mr. Carpenter and Dr. Lewis went to El Cayo at once to prepare for the autopsy; I stayed behind to see that the body was properly transported.

The dugout canoe which carried it to El Cayo was manned by a crew of four experienced men who knew the river and its rapids and whom I trusted to make the voyage in safety.

The body arrived in El Cayo at 8:00 P.M., where Dr. Lewis performed the autopsy at once. The autopsy consumed two hours, and when we entered the cemetery, it was ten o'clock. Father Hermann, S.J., met us at the grave and read the Roman Catholic burial service, and this brief ceremony closed the long sad day. That same night I dispatched my wireless message notifying you of the matter.

1918

VOYAGE TO TULUUM

Morley was of the opinion that during the height of the Maya "Old Empire" (ca. 100 B.C. to A.D. 600) several colonization movements spread from the Petén lowlands into the northern Yucatán Peninsula. Dated monuments at a chain of ancient centers appeared to him to support such an hypothesis, one thrust moving along the western side of the peninsula and the other along the eastern coast. He felt that neither colonization was a potent one, for the cities left behind were neither numerous nor large, but that the structures of the east coast seemed more reminiscent of those of the Petén area than did those of the western coast. More recent research indicates, however, that these areas had a synchronous cultural development to that taking place in the more southerly lowlands which may have been of equal, rather than satellite, status. The fact that the east coast cities more resemble those of the Petén is due in part to the isolation of the district, the occupied areas of the immediate hinterland away from the littoral having been abandoned probably several centuries before the collapse of the Petén centers which created an empty belt that effectively cut this region off from later developments. Furthermore, this east coast was more extensively occupied in ancient times than early workers believed had been the case. Certainly towns here appear to have been in use until much later times than elsewhere.

One of the most intriguing Classic period cities of the eastern Yucatán coast is Tuluum, which because of its defensive location on a cliff above the blue waters of the Caribbean varies somewhat in appearance from most other ancient Maya settlements. However, it has corbelled roof vaults, wall paintings, and at least two stelae bearing Initial Series date glyphs, one of which is as early as the end of the sixth century. In spite of these dates, its greatest occupation appears to have come late in the Postclassic period ("New Empire" to Morley), with some indications of the central Mexican influence which had been so strong at Chichén Itzá.

Tuluum has been known since the Juan de Grijalva expedition of 1518 when the Spaniards sailed along the shore after leaving their landfall at the island of Cozumel. However, since that time the entire Yucatán east coast area has remained a little known region because of a dearth of natural resources which might have brought in modern means of transportation. It is a physiographic province of low scrub forest, mangrove and salt swamps, limestone outcroppings, and a dangerous coastline which lies in a hurricane path. Furthermore, during the last century eastern Yucatán and Quintana Roo have been refuge areas for rebellious Maya who fled the henequen and sugar plantations of Yucatán during the long Caste War, loosely but fiercely united under a fanatic religious cult, and fought off Emperor Maximilian's army and then that of the Mexican Republic. These rebel Maya established a capital at a forest settlement inland from Ascensión Bay which they called Chan Santa Cruz because of the location there of a Speaking Cross which was the mouthpiece for their sect. In 1902 the Cruzob, or People of the Cross, finally were defeated by Porfirio Díaz's army, the town was renamed Santa Cruz de Bravo, after the conquering general, and the huge church structure begun by the Maya was converted to a prison. Ultimately the Mexican troops withdrew, the Maya dispersed back into the forests, and the area—which never had been capable of supporting a concentrated population—further declined economically.

In 1913 Morley made his first trip to Tuluum. Subsequently, in 1916 he returned in the company of Samuel Lothrop of Harvard University. The following journal excerpts, taken from a 1918 diary, tell of his third visit, just four hundred years after the discovery of Tuluum. As will become apparent, the main purpose of the trip was to recover an Initial Series glyph which had been cached away several seasons previously. The earliness of the date was then considered an incongruity which could not be explained because Morley and others believed Tuluum post dated the twelfth century League of Mayapán. However, the Initial Series date now has been accepted as indicative of foundation prior to the Postclassic development which had flourished in the region.

As part of a plan to try to visit all Yucatán sites known to have glyphs, in the spring of 1918 Morley, together with an artist named John Held, Jr., and Thomas Gann, a British colonial doctor who was also an avid archaeologist, again chartered a small boat at Belize to carry them northward, eventually to skirt the wild, practically deserted Yucatán coastline. The account picks up at the great Ascensión Bay of Quintana Roo.

February 8, Friday
It seemed doubtful that we could make Ascensión Bay and get through the reef there before nightfall, but we decided to make a try for it. We dropped the pilot at Punta Herrera and put out through the reef. The sea was raising the devil outside. The sunlight on the blue waters of the Gulf Stream was lovely, but great high rollers kept coming in. Presently my stomach was

quite upset and so continued for close on to five hours until we anchored off Culebra Keys in the mouth of the bay.

The Mexican government formerly had a settlement of convicts on the largest of these keys, but these fellows built a raft in 1911 and escaped to the mainland. It has been unoccupied ever since. The southernmost key, off which we now found ourselves, had a few fishermen's huts. After getting our cots and bedding together into the jolly boat, we put off for the shore.

After going aground once or twice, we finally landed. The fishermen were natives of the colony of San Pedro on Ambergris Key, five old men and every one over fifty-five. They made us welcome in their simple fashion and offered us the use of their house, but we preferred to sleep outside.

Muddy [servant] put the cots up behind their house and then returned to the Lilian Y. John [Held, artist] never sleeps ashore as he has become quite accustomed to the motion of the sea.

We talked to the five old men, who were fishers and turtlers, for nearly an hour before turning in. Then bidding them goodnight, we betook ourselves to our cots, dodged under our mosquito nettings and went to bed.

Sometime during the night, Gann [medical officer of British Honduras], annoyed by the snoring of the San Pedronos within the hut, moved his cot to a more silent locality, but the noise did not break my rest.

February 9, Saturday

Muddy came ashore for us early. Taking leave of these pleasant men, who really appeared to be enjoying themselves in this lonesome though delightful little key, we returned to the Lilian Y. The captain got the boat under way. While we were crossing the six miles from this key to Ascensión, we had breakfast. As we were approaching the point, a small sailing vessel flying the Mexican flag sailed across our bows and told us to halt. She had the Custom House official on her, and he came aboard. When he saw General Solis's letters, he put himself at our disposition. So we towed him into his port.

Ascensión, originally a place of some twenty-five hundred souls, was founded by General de la Vega in 1902 as a military camp from which the pacification of Quintana Roo was attempted. After Santa Cruz de Bravo was established, Ascensión lost its importance and fell into decay. The cyclone of two years ago felled most of the houses and just about wiped it off the map. It has now dwindled to eight persons—the lighthouse keeper, his family, and two minor Customs officials. There is even no commandante, and Heaven knows, the town in these countries which cannot boast a commandante is indeed in a bad way.

There was little to see ashore: the lighthouse, which is no tower but only a steel frame, up and down which slides the light; the aduana [customs house] and a dilapidated Cinco de Mayo iron arch [May 5, a Mexican national holiday to celebrate the Puebla defeat of French forces in 1862]. I took a few photographs. Then we returned to the wharf and put out.

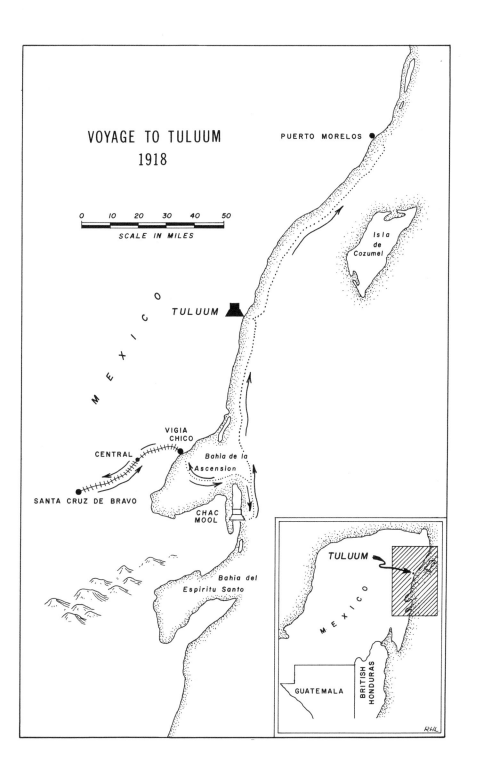

VOYAGE TO TULUUM
1918

PUERTO MORELOS ●

0   10   20   30   40   50
SCALE IN MILES

Isla
de
Cozumel

M E X I C O

TULUUM ▲

VIGIA
CHICO

CENTRAL

Bahia de la
Ascension

SANTA CRUZ DE BRAVO

CHAC
MOOL

Bahia del
Espiritu Santo

TULUUM

M E X I C O

GUATEMALA

BRITISH
HONDURAS

RHL

There was a Belize creole here by the name of Peter Moguel who had lived in the vicinity for some fifteen years and was of more than the average intelligence. He knew the bay and its channels, as well as the road to Santa Cruz de Bravo, so I engaged him by the day until we should leave hereabouts. We set off across the bay for Vigia Chico, the tidewater terminus of the railroad to Santa Cruz de Bravo.

Vigia Chico, next to Xcalac, seems to have suffered most heavily from the cyclone of 1916. Freight cars were tipped off the wharf into the shallow water of the bay; a barge driven a quarter of a mile inshore; and houses galore blown completely over or caved in. It presented a scene of great desolation.

Muddy rigged up the Evinrude in the jolly boat, and we went ashore. All the male population, some fifty odd men, were waiting on the wharf. Peter proved very useful here by introducing us to the military officer and the main chicle operator of the region, Don Julio Martín, a Cuban.

Walking ahead with these leading citizens, we moved along the wharf. We wanted to visit Santa Cruz de Bravo and to do so it was necessary to arrange the matter with Don Julio who was the only one having mules. He had good news for us indeed: General Francisco Mai, head chief of all the east coast Maya, is due tomorrow at Central, a station up the line, to arrange with Don Julio's assistant there about milpa lands for the coming season.

On hearing this, we decided to leave at once for Central. While Don Julio was arranging for mules, Gann and I returned to the ship where John had remained. There followed an orgy of packing. Everybody wanted to be in the hold at the same time, which was a physical impossibility.

After two hours hard work, we emerged from the boat with a great mass of impedimenta, with probably everything forgotten that we will really need. We had tea and crackers before leaving and then returned via the jolly boat to the land.

The small trucks were ready, a mule for each, and when the baggage was quickly loaded on them, we set off.

This railroad is a narrow Decauville affair, two inch gauge with about twenty pound rails. It was built from Vigia Chico to Santa Cruz de Bravo, fifty-six kilometers inland, which was to have the double purpose of serving as a military base from which to conquer the independent Maya of the east coast and as a penal colony for the whole of the republic. Indeed the railroad, such as it is, was built by convict labor. It was started by General de la Vega in 1902 and later given over to General Ignacio Bravo, an old companion of Porfirio Díaz.

Bravo had visions of making Vigia the port of Yucatán, taking the chicle business from Progreso, and the town which, under the name of Chan Santa Cruz, dates from the Spanish period was rechristened Santa Cruz de Bravo in his honor.

It was distinctly a military occupation of the country, and the railroad was only for military purposes. The bush for thirty meters on either side of the right of way had to be kept cleared as a no man's land to prevent the Santa Cruz Indians from attacking the trains as they passed.

After the Madero revolution in 1910 and after Bravo left in 1911, the place fell into decay. In August, 1915, General Alvarado, then Governor of Yûcatán, ordered its abandonment.

The line was cut for slightly under a mile between kilometers nine and eleven. It was necessary to transfer our baggage from the trucks to the backs of the mules and walk across this break. In this shuffle I got changed to the forward car and rode the rest of the way to Central by myself.

The country is poor beyond words. The native limestone crops out everywhere, grudgingly contesting with the sparse low bush of the region its very right to exist. Yet low as the bush is, it is impenetrably thick and thorny.

Central is a miserable place filled with miserable Mexican chicleros. The encargador, Don Rosendo Vila, a Spaniard, was a good fellow, and made us comfortable.

We had dinner in a lamina house amid a riot of flea-scratching dogs and cats. Don Rosendo is expecting General Mai tomorrow about noon. So we decided to go on to Santa Cruz de Bravo early in the morning, returning to Central in the early afternoon to meet the general.

Gann elected to sleep outside, as he said the dogs and snoring would prevent him from sleeping. John and I slept inside. It was awful. Chicleros were expectorating all night long, dogs were investigating fleas, and there was snoring and uncanny noises. It rained heavily toward morning and drove Gann inside dripping water and ill-temper. His face, as he wrote at the table in the light of a flickering hurricane lantern, was a study in utter and abandoned disgust.

February 10, Sunday

It was morning at last, and we got up nothing loath to leave our beds. We took only cameras, notebooks, and John's sketching material and set off at a good pace, all packed on one truck.

The railroad lay through the same poor country as yesterday. It was easy to see why the Maya had never occupied it intensively. At Station D, kilometer 42, we saw a few mounds in the no man's land on the south side of of the track. These were so low and so casual that from the track we could not decide whether they were artificial or natural. About here we got a good drenching, which added to our discomfort.

Long before making kilometer 49, where the track has been torn up for two kilometers, the mule called La Grandota because of its large size, began to show signs of fatigue or laziness. Arriving at kilometer 49, we left our truck and walked on to kilometer 51, where the track begins again and where Don Rosendo said we would find another truck. The driver brought the

Grandota along so that we could ride the last seven kilometers to Santa Cruz. But things fell out differently.

When we got to the track on the other side, we found no truck. Don Rosendo said the Indians still living at Santa Cruz must have carried it thither; so we were obliged to walk these last seven kilometers.

Peter set out at a brisk gait, followed by John, Don Rosendo, and me. It began to rain just then, and Gann and Muddy stayed behind. We were drenched from the hard rain which lasted half an hour.

It was after eleven when the track turned to the right and ran into the town. What ruin and desolation! Although abandoned but yesterday, already the bush was running over its plazas, streets, and buildings. In the outskirts we passed falling wooden houses, an expensive gas engine rusted and worthless, sagging water tanks. Here was the machine shop, its roof falling, bushes growing in the doorway and hiding the entrance, and within rust and ruin. Farther on we passed "The Club," another ruin. After several streets filled with a ten foot growth of bush and young saplings, we caught sight of the immense barrel vault of the church, a relic of the Spanish period, and turning again to the right, we entered the plaza. The fountain was choked with weeds, and the water supply dried up. Formerly this was supplied by an expensive pumping plant.

The plaza, also dating from Spanish times, is filled with an orchard of sour orange trees, the only thriving thing about the city. The cement walks are now hidden in long grass, and the central kiosk is in ruins.

At one corner of the plaza stands the church which has had a remarkable history, going back to Spanish times for its foundation, I believe possibly even to the seventeenth century. It was never finished; it lacks its towers, and the facade never has had any decoration.

In 1848 when all this part of Yucatán was abandoned because of the War of the Castes, the Santa Cruz Indians who occupied the place made of this church a kind of Maya delphic oracle. The cross here is said to have had a hole in it through which a concealed person could give responses. Prisoners of war were thus brought before the "Santa Cruz" to learn their fate. The fame attained a great local celebrity.

When the Mexicans reoccupied the town under General Bravo about 1905, the Indians carried off the Santa Cruz to their settlement in the bush. The Mexicans used the church as a prison, herding as many as two hundred prisoners—men, women, and children—into it at one time. Terrible scenes were there enacted. The convicts, the very street sweepings of Mexico, would quarrel, fight, and even kill in the shadow of the high altar. It was, in short, a bloody pestilential charnel house under the Mexican regime. Few religious edifices can boast a history equal to this: church, pagan oracle, and prison house, in three successive centuries, and now again an abandoned ruin with staring open doorways and dark gloomy interior.

Happily for the prisoners incarcerated there, the church is large, one hundred five feet long inside, and thirty-six feet wide, with ceiling fully seventy-five feet high and walls eight feet thick. To offset this, there are no windows save one large one in the front, and except for three large doorways there are no other openings in the walls. The interior is correspondingly dark and gloomy.

Portales dating from the Spanish period adjoin the church on either side, used for quarters in the Mexican occupation of the town. These bore every mark of hasty abandonment. A cart left here, a table there, and now the bush growing everywhere.

Across the Calle de Libertad from the quarters was the house of General Bravo, a hideous wooden affair of two stories, fast falling to pieces. Opposite the church was another colonnaded building of the Spanish period used by the Mexicans for a hospital. And beyond for a considerable distance were ruined buildings on all sides. It was a veritable city of the dead.

At its height in the Mexican occupation (1905-1915), the town boasted close to three thousand persons. In the Spanish period, judging from the large church and ample colonnades, it can hardly have been less large. Now two families of Santa Cruz Indians, less than a dozen people, are the only human beings who waken the echoes in its deserted streets. Of the two occupations, Spanish and Mexican, the latter in a few years will have left far less trace than the former.

We photographed and sketched amid these ruins until word came that lunch was ready at the house of one of the Indians. We had a delicious tomato omelet, ground corn mixed with hot water and salt, some peppers, and many hot tortillas which the wife of the Indian made while we waited. After taking a photograph of this Maya family, we climbed aboard the truck and started back to Central.

The mule had not grown any stronger during our stay at Santa Cruz. It took us an interminable time to get back to the break at kilometer 51-49, but this was as nothing compared to those fifteen kilometers that were beyond. We tried every means of making the wretched beast go forward—cajolery, persuasion, coercion, profanity, and flagellation—but nothing availed. Indeed, under direct corporal punishment of the most violent sort, it would stop dead in its tracks and refuse to move. We calculated afterward that we averaged from two to two and three-quarters miles an hour.

In consequence of the slowness of this mule, we reached Central only just before sunset. We found that General Mai had not arrived, nor in fact had been heard from.

February 11, Monday

Don Rosendo had told us yesterday of a Catholic cemetery in the bush just behind Station D, with tombs standing and a cross on top of one of them. We were at a loss to account for a Spanish cemetery so far from anywhere, about eight miles from the nearest Spanish town known, Santa Cruz, and so with the hope of possibly getting a date on one of the tombstones, Gann and I decided to visit the place during the morning while we were waiting for General Mai to show up. We decided that if he did not get in by noon, he would not get in at all, and we would return in the afternoon to Vigia Chico.

The mule we had was full of life. What it had taken us an hour and forty-five minutes to do yesterday, we now did in forty-five minutes.

We left the mule and car at Station D and set off across the milpa south of the tracks. On the edge of the no man's land we examined a mound of crude stone construction, which we decided was Maya, not Spanish. While we were looking this over, Don Rosendo had been hunting around in the bush. He called to us that he had found the tomb. We followed a trail he had made and soon came to one of the most perfect little Maya temples I have ever seen. It was two stories high and stood on a low platform. All three levels combined are slightly under nine feet high. The second story stood on the on the first like a smaller block stands on a large one.

It was almost perfect; in fact, it lacked only the cross, which Don Rosendo said had formerly stood on the summit. Unfortunately, no trace of this remained, it having been destroyed by the soldiers of General Ribera who founded Station D. We regretted this latter circumstance since a Maya temple surmounted by a Christian cross would be a treasure trove. I rather doubted that there had ever been a cross. Not that Don Rosendo was deceiving us at all, but he might have mistaken a purely Maya ornament like the frets at Chichén, for example, for a cross. However, the ornament was destroyed, and speculation was useless.

We photographed the temple, measured it, and set out to see a few others. These had been thrown down by the Mexican soldiers so that no one was entire.

Returning to the no man's land, we passed an aguada, which had been artificially formed or modified. It was perhaps a hundred feet across and doubtless served as the water supply of the ancient city.

We started back for Central at a good pace and were there in forty minutes. John had spent a busy morning in painting, having three pictures in his book. Muddy had the packing all done when we got back, and after lunch, General Mai not having come, we set about returning to Vigia Chico.

We had gone as far as kilometer 28, four kilometers before the point where the trail from General Mai's capital comes in, when we saw two Indians walking up the track. When we got close enough to recognize them, Peter and the driver said the man was Desiderio Cochua, General Mai's first captain. We stopped, and with Muddy acting as interpreter, had a long talk.

The reason the general had not come was because he was ill with chills and fever. Here was Gann's opportunity. He got out his bag and gave the first captain some quinine and cough mixture. Muddy explained we were bearing gifts for the general and looking for ruins. At our direction he asked the man if he knew of any ruins behind Tuluum. To our great delight, he said there was a good sized place two leagues from Tuluum which was even larger than Tuluum.

We brought down the gramophone at this, told him it was for the general, and played it to him from the end of a railroad tie. Gann showed him the photograph taken in Belize of their friends, and he was greatly pleased. Through Muddy we made an agreement to meet him next Saturday the 16th, at Tuluum. He was to get General Mai to come if possible, but if not, he was to come anyhow. Giving him some cigars and cigarettes as an earnest of our good faith and future intentions, and to the nice looking little Maya boy who accompanied him, some chocolate candy, we bid them good-bye and mounting the car, set off.

February 14, Thursday

I found out yesterday that our new pilot knew where the large "Spanish ruins" were between Ascensión and Espiritu Santo Bays, the group that poor old Peter Vásquez had told me of several years ago. His account of these was so glowing that even at the cost of putting back on our course sixty-four miles we decided to go back and visit them. We thought by getting cleared last night we could get off at 7:00 this morning and make the point of Santa Rosa, where Miguel said the ruins were located, before nightfall. The delay of an hour and a half beyond this schedule prevented us from carrying out the plan.

All day long we pushed the Lilian Y, but current and wind were both against us. As dusk came on, Miguel said we could not make Santa Rosa before dark. So I told him to go as far as he could, but to be sure to get us inside the bay before night fell as I was too seasick to sleep aboard.

The sun set, but still the old man held out to open sea. I began urging him to go in, but he held his course, but finally just as dusk crept on, we slipped through the reef to everyone's great relief and came to anchor a quarter of a mile off shore. As soon as the anchor dropped, we made immediate preparations for going ashore. A new moon hung in the sky and presaged better nights to come, but for the present it was darker than Egypt. Finally we got off in the jolly boat, and landed in the usual scurrying manner, getting half wet as always.

As the cots and nets were fixed, Gann discovered a fresh jaguar spoor passing up the beach right by our beds! These were fairly large and very fresh. It seemed wisest to have arms by us in the event this feline returned. So we sent the boys off for some artillery. They fetched back Gann's shotgun and my 45 automatic revolver. I slept with one eye open, but nothing untoward happened to break our rest. The jaguar must have returned by some other route.

February 15, Friday

We just got aboard in the morning in time to catch a heavy shower.

This had been brewing since daylight and broke after breakfast just as we were getting under way. The heaviest part of it passed off to the southwest and before we reached Santa Rosa, it had cleared. We were scarcely an hour between Xnoku Point and Santa Rosa. An hour more of daylight would have brought us to our destination last night instead of this morning.

We went ashore and had a cold breakfast under a small coconut tree before setting out for the ruins. Five of us went: Gann, John, me, Muddy, and Miguel. Gann was more cheerful than usual: felt we had lost two days, gone one hundred twenty miles out of our way, and burned God knows how many gallons of oil, all for nothing. This philosophy had one indisputable advantage: anything that turns out at all favorable, however small and insignificant, is all velvet.

We set off down the beach for nearly a mile. The unfrequented character of this shore was revealed in the amount of valuable wreckage strewing the beach. Here a mahogany log of value, there a dory, cars, life preservers, lumber, and other valuable salvage material.

We climbed a bank of sand dunes and turned into the bush. Everywhere the salt water pimento predominated. After wrestling with the bush for some time, we came out on a mud flat near the long arm of Ascensión Bay which extends to the south. It bore the marks of deer everywhere.

After ten minutes of this more open going, we turned into the bush again. Miguel said he thought we were in the vicinity of the church. After stumbling around in the pimento bush for fifteen minutes, he decided he was on the wrong trail and put back to the mud flats.

Here we let him and Muddy do the scouting while we rested behind. We were already tired and perspiring from fighting the bush. Muddy said they would fire off a gun if they found the church.

We had been resting about half an hour when we heard a shot not far off to the south. Soon the men returned with the news that a ruined city had been found but not the big church Miguel had seen eight years ago when he was hunting deer. We set off through the bush and presently crossed a low dance platform and found ourselves in front of a small temple of the Tuluum type. We went quickly from this to three or four others, one mounted on a pyramid perhaps fifteen feet high. Then we had a council of war at the base of the last.

It was obviously a new Maya city of no little importance. We had already seen enough to keep us busy for a day in mapping and photographing it, and besides there was some clearing necessary for the latter. We decided to send Muddy back to the boat to bring out as many of the crew as extra pay would attract, with axes and machetes, and lunch for us. Miguel went back with him to the playa to open up a trail directly from the beach to the ruins. This was much shorter than wandering around through the mud flats.

While they were gone, the three of us started on the map of the site and were so energetic that by the time Muddy returned with the lunch and the men, we had it half done, including the ground plans and elevations of four temples.

Before eating, I put the boys, five of whom responded to the call to arms, to work cutting down the bush and trees in front of the principal temple. This had one important and unique feature which I think I have never seen before, namely, an arch or formal gateway approaching it. To be sure, the arcade idea is old. Witness the House of the Pigeons and the south range of the Monjas at Uxmal or the Portal at Labna. Even the independent arch is not entirely unique as there is one at Kabah. But an arch leading directly to a temple was new to me. Moreover, this proved to have an entirely new feature in a Chac Mool figure reclining on the floor of this arch directly in the line of approach to the main temple above. [Chac Mool figures are of central Mexican origin and are an indication of foreign, probably Toltec, influence upon this region.] Alfredo uncovered its knees first and then the hands along the thighs before I discovered that it was a Chac Mool. Going deeper, the boys exposed the breast, arms, and shoulders. The head unhappily was broken off, although we found a fragment showing part of the left eye, left ear plug, the forehead and headdress. By this time it was nearly five. We decided to knock off work for the day to return tomorrow with picks and shovel to complete the disinterment of the Chac Mool. We returned to the playa well satisfied with the result of the day's work. The boys went back to the Lilian Y and brought her down to where our path emerged from the bush. We went aboard for supper and then came ashore for the night.

It looked so much like rain that we pitched our cots in the pimento grove on the sand dunes and had the tarpaulin stretched above them. Mindful of the tiger's tracks of last night, we had a lantern put on the head of each bed and, as an extra precaution, our firearms under them. It rained briskly in the night but not a drop came through the tarp, though misery-loving Gann claimed to have sustained wet feet.

February 16, Saturday

We went aboard for breakfast since for once the Lilian Y was anchored nearby, and got off early for the ruins with three or four of the crew carrying picks and shovels. Before leaving, I had Miguel and George climb the mast to see whether there might be any eminences rising from the plain which might be Miguel's still-missing church. George reported a higher hill than any we had yet seen not far south of the main group. When we reached the ruins, Miguel set out to try to locate it.

John put Alfredo and George to work digging out the Chac Mool, and Gann and I finished the general map. Presently Miguel returned with the report of another large ruined building. Gann and I went over to look at it. It proved to be one of those tremendous colonnaded halls like the two at Tuluum which are one hundred two feet long. [Colonnades are another central Mexican feature.] In its entirety it must have presented a fine appearance. Now with the roof fallen and over half its columns prostrate, it was the apogee of ruin and desolation.

To return to the Chac Mool. By this time John had it completely uncovered and ready for photographing. Several interesting objects had been found during the course of this work; a fine little incensario with a head on it, a triangular shell gorget, several beads, and an excellent jade ear plug. The Chac Mool himself was an object of wonder and interest. He was of extraordinary height, or would have been if erect: seven feet. He was sixty-six inches around the chest and nineteen inches around the biceps, almost heroic in size. The head was turned ninety degrees to the left as in all figures of this type, and the hands rested against the thighs. There was no receptacle in the abdomen or chest for incense, as in the famous one from Chichén Itzá. The figure was made of stucco and had been painted. Lying thus in the deserted forest, headless and alone, he seemed forever doomed to contemplate the desolation of his shrine and the destruction of his worshippers.

This figure was easily the most important object in the city, both as to location and characteristics. We gave the place its name: Chac Mool, though future explorers should note it is about one-fifth of a mile in from the playa just north of the point known locally as Santa Rosa.

We finished photographing the principal temples and measured the large colonnaded hall. Then we returned to the playa. On the way out, we passed a small square temple near the shore.

Gann had already preceded us on board. As soon as we reached the Lilian Y, we set off about one. When we passed Xnoku Point, near where we had slept night before last, we put in through the reef again.

I went ashore with Miguel, Alfredo, George, and Kuylen to see the ruins of the Spanish church said to be there. Instead I found a nice little Maya temple with two columns. Its eastern end had been entirely destroyed. Formerly there had been another temple just in front of it, but this had been completely destroyed by fishermen to make sinkers for their dories. Indeed, the other temple was speedily sharing the same fate.

As soon as I returned to the boat, we weighed anchor and put out through the reef again. We hoped to be able to make that delightful beach at Boca Paila where we put Peter Moguel ashore, but the sun set just as we got beyond Allen Point. We had to put in through the reef only three miles above Ascensión light. Gann and I slept on the beach as usual, John remaining aboard.

February 17, Sunday

A double disappointment today. But all that in its proper place. We got a good start, but it was nearly 11:00 before we were finally abreast of Tuluum. As we passed through the break in the reef, where we so nearly had a disastrous ending two years ago, an accident occurred which but for the exceptionally fine weather we have been enjoying might easily have proved fatal to all aboard.

Just as we were passing between the jaws of the reef, the engine suddenly stopped dead. Alfredo, who was on deck, dived into the companion-way and tried to resuscitate it but without success. In this delicate position, we drifted for a moment, the teeth of the reef not twenty-five yards from us on either side. Happily the captain, who was at the wheel, had his wits about him and hastily ordered the sails up. With scarcely enough wind to fill them, we drifted through this dangerous break and came to anchor in the scarcely less smooth waters within!

Of all the places on the east coast of Yucatán, Tuluum has the worst name among mariners. Here, even on the calmest days, a heavy surf pounds the rockbound coast, due, our pilot said, to the strong current which is always running. Certainly this has been my experience. In 1913, in 1916, and now in 1918 a heavy surf has been rolling in.

We scanned the Castillo anxiously for signs of Desiderio Cahau but there was no sign of life about the tower or its platform. As it was not yet high noon, we decided to eat lunch before going ashore.

Five of us put off in the first boat: Gann, John, me, George and Kuylen. The water was breaking too fiercely in the bight to permit our entering there, so we made for the beach just under the high cliffs south of the Castillo. We felt our way in very carefully and anchored the jolly boat outside the breakers in three feet of water. From here, Kuylen and George carried us in on their backs. John felt miserable and faint and lay down in the shade of the cliff to pull himself together.

After resting a bit ourselves, Gann and I climbed the cliff, entered the salt water pimento bush on top, and beat our way around through the plaza in front of the Castillo and down the other side to the bight where we had left the stela two years ago. Miguel joined us here. I came out on the beach first, and, to my consternation, could not see the stela. I called out this disconcerting news to Gann, who could not believe me. We both were so sure Peter Vásquez had not taken it.

It was a great blow. After giving the beach careful scrutiny, we sat down to mourn this missing treasure. We visualized it at the bottom of the Caribbean in the hold of Peter's sunken craft. Miguel, however, was sure this could not be. He knew Peter well, he said, was his "compadre," and said that on Peter's last voyage he never got beyond Ascensión Bay. Miguel said his partner had gone to Cozumel and had returned with a Mexican official on board with an order for Peter's arrest. Miguel and this partner had smuggled Peter off to Puerto Herrera, from where he had departed for Xcalak. Later he was overtaken by the great cyclone of October, 1916, and drowned. Miguel capped this argument with the statement that Peter had offered him fifty dollars gold to put into Tuluum to get the stela.

We developed five possible fates that could have overtaken the monument: 1) that Peter had carried it off in some way and that it was therefore lost forever; 2) that some one of the thousand other people Gann has sent for it from time to time had called for it and carried it off; 3) that the Indians, seeing our activities of two years ago, had themselves carried it off into the bush for reasons best known to themselves; 4) that the sea in the great cyclone of two years ago had either washed it out to sea or destroyed it; or finally 5) that it lay buried in the sand which the cyclone appeared to have washed in.

We determined to dig the next morning all around where we had left the stela. With this faint hope, we returned to the beach and went aboard the Lilian Y to bring our living impedimenta back ashore.

This was no slight task because we planned to transfer our cooking establishment ashore, and also because of the difficulty of landing through the high surf. John and I went in with the first boat load, carrying our beds and bedding, and had the boys haul them up the cliff to the Castillo where we had decided to sleep.

Gann came in with the second and last load, which comprised the cooking outfit and food. He climbed the Castillo cursing like a trooper and drenched to the skin. It seems he had the boys come in too far, and a wave broke over the stern of the jolly boat to wet him through.

I put George to burning off the brush on the terrace in front of the Castillo. He commenced by cutting down one of those thorny bushes in which ants inhabit the thorns. After he had scattered an army of these about, and, as he expressed it, after they had "put heat into the flesh" by biting everybody, I had him desist. Thorns were preferable to these devilish ants.

Meanwhile Hubert and Muddy were getting supper. After this meal, the boys put up our cots and then returned to the boat for the night. None of them wanted to sleep on shore because of the Indians.

Gann had elected to sleep outside on the terrace, but John and I chose the outer corridor of the temple proper, John in his hammock and I on my cot.

The moon was magnificent, and we sat on the terrace discussing subjects appropriate to the time and place: the age of the ruins, scenes that must have been enacted where we were so quietly conversing at that very moment, of Stephens [John Stephens, explorer among the ruins in 1842] whose trail we were again crossing. Before going to bed we went around behind the temple, which overlooks the sea, to watch the moon light up the water with its silvery radiance. At our feet the surf broke white against the base of the cliff, and so extended a ribbon of white on the sea of silver up and down as far as the eye could reach. The Lilian Y lay at anchor with her top light twinkling back and forth in the heavy swell, which made me very thankful I was not aboard her.

It rained in the night, and Gann was obliged to come inside. I helped him in with his bed, which we put up in the inner chamber.

February 18, Monday

Alfredo and his boy came ashore to work for us. After breakfast, we all went down to the beach to set them digging up the sand where we had left the stela. It was a slender hope,but all we could do under the circumstances.

Leaving them under John's direction, who said he would boss the job while he made water colors of the bight, I went off with Miguel to make a complete circuit of the walls. Gann disappeared to look up some wall paintings. Miguel and I went first to the sea end of the north wall and then started westward. When we came to the first passage, I stopped at the building there over the cenote of brackish water to take the measurements for its ground plan. I think Sam Lothrop failed to secure these two years ago.

After this, we continued on around the north wall, noting the other passage therein, and on to the tower at the northwest corner. Thence we walked across the back to the passage through it and beyond to the southwest corner and the other tower.

When we reached here, it was nearly 1:00. Faintly through the woods we could hear the others hallooing for us to come to dinner. So we set out for the Castillo, arriving there fifteen minutes later, hot and tired from fighting the thorny bush all morning.

Here good and bad news awaited us. No Desiderio had shown up. We forthwith abandoned all hopes of seeing him. And better tidings, John had found four of the seven missing stela fragments. These were recovered within twenty-five feet of each other, scattered along the edge of the bush, presumably where the sea had thrown them in the cyclone of two years ago.

This considerably heartened us all, and gave hope that further search would reveal the big top piece which carried the Initial Series. The other two fragments were very small, and I feared they would not be recovered.

After lunch Gann took Muddy down to look for the still missing fragments, while Miguel and I set off for the east, or sea, end of the south wall. We measured the two passages through this, then followed the wall to the southwest corner, the point at which we had quit before lunch. This wall is clearly of a defensive character. It abuts on the steep cliff running down to the sea at each end and encloses an area of twenty-two acres. The north and south walls are six hundred fifty feet long, the west, or land, wall fifteen hundred feet long. It varies in height, owing to the rolling nature of the ground, from six to eighteen feet and from fifteen to twenty-five, and in one place at the southwest corner is thirty-seven feet in thickness. It has a parapet all the way around the outside and behind this a platform six feet above the level of the ground inside the enclosure. Both the outer and inner sides of this massive construction rise at a steep batter. The stones used are rough and show little or no signs of dressing. They appear to have been dry laid into the wall.

The five passageways are narrow, not more than four feet wide and six to seven feet high. The eastern one in the north wall, that near the guard house of the cenote, had an offset in it which must have greatly facilitated its defense. It seemed clear to me why the enclosure was so large. In case of attack the entire tribe could be assembled within the walls. Here was water and here doubtless were ample stores of corn. Behind these strong fortifications the city was practially impregnable against any attack.

Believing as I do that all these cities of the east coast were not founded until after the fall of Mayapan circa A.D. 1441, when all centralized authority in the peninsula broke down and every tribe was warring with its neighbor, such defenses were necessary. The prince of Tuluum made himself as secure as he could against the vicissitudes and uncertainties of his epoch.

When Miguel and I had finished the wall, we beat back northward along the west wall to the northwest corner and there, spreading out fan wise, started toward the sea to try to locate the three buildings Sam Lothrop and Arthur Carpenter thought they had noted in this corner of the enclosure. I had hoped we might not find these as I was tired of measuring in such a thicket, but luck was against me. About fifty feet south of the western passageway in the north wall I found them: two dance platforms and a temple. One of the former had a very small house on it. The other was unusual in having a parapet entirely around it. The temple had an interesting small inner shrine, as well as a little back door, a sort of privy entrance which, I fancy, the priests found useful in slipping into the holy of holies from behind without the faithful in front knowing about it.

The bush was very thick hereabouts. Indeed at some not distant time, it had been completely cleared just east of these three constructions but had grown back very thick.

Before we had finished clearing these structures, I heard Gann calling. Being bent on the same errand as we, he and Muddy presently came crashing through the bush in trying to discover these same three buildings.

When I had completed their measurement, we returned to the bight to look at the recovered fragments of the stela. Muddy had found the big top piece buried in the sand not far from where we had left it. Now only two small fragments were missing.

I scrutinized the side opposite the Initial Series carefully for glyphs of any sort which would bring the troublesome early Initial Series 9.6.10.0.0 8 *Ahau* 13 *Pax* [A.D. 564] forward to a more historically probable period, and not without some measure of success. In one place was a coefficient of 7 attached to a day sign and following the lahuntun sign. This enabled us to supply the effaced day sign as *Ahau.* Again on the opposite column of glyphs the day 7 *Ahau* after a tun sign was unmistakably recorded. What did this mean—a record of the day 7 *Ahau* ending a lahuntun when the Initial Series day was so clearly 8 *Ahau?*

It occurred to me that in the next cycle the lahuntun 10.6.10.0.0 might end on the day 7 *Ahau.* Gann and I sat down on the beach, took out our notebooks, and fell to work on the necessary calculations to find this out. As usual in such cases, these dates never work out right the first time owing to some footling error in one's arithmetic. So we both reached different results and neither the day 7 *Ahau*. However, on a second trial we both got 7 *Ahau,* the day recorded, and we tucked away the result as promising.

After this, we all took a bath in the sea and then returned to the Castillo, where the boys had supper ready. This was almost a sacrament, as we had killed our pet and only hen, which we had carried with us all the way from Corozal. The poor creature was losing weight. Rather than abandon her way in the bush to be killed by some beast of prey, we gave a reluctant consent to have her killed and served for dinner last night. Muddy refused outright to do the fell work, and Hubert was none too anxious. We ate the last of her at supper, and I must confess relished her greatly.

And still no Desiderio. We decided to wait no longer for him but to leave the first thing in the morning.

Again in the evening we sat on the terrace under a wonderful moon and talked archaeology. Our thoughts turned instinctively to the stela. We discussed the possibility of the new evidence declaring the contemporaneous date of the monument.

It seemed as though it might. Chichén Itzá was abandoned in 10.3.0.0.0 [A.D. 889, the last Initial Series date from the site but prior to the great Maya-Toltec period which was responsible for many of the best preserved structures at the city] and seventy years later a stela may have been set up here, i.e. in 10.6.10.0.0 7 *Ahau* 8 *Yaxkin* [A.D. 958]. We held this hypothesis up to every angle of criticism we could level against it and only laid it aside at bed time without having developed any flaw therein.

This morning the boys killed a small snake of a very poisonous variety in the stones of the cornice of the Castillo. It was with some misgivings, therefore, that I finally climbed into my bed. It seemed to me I remembered an old superstition to the effect that snakes, like everything else, are usually found in pairs.

Gann, in spite of his wetting of last night, elected to sleep outside again.

February 19, Tuesday

As soon as the boys came ashore, we started them carrying our beds and bedding down to the beach. We had finished with Tuluum for this time, all but for one thing: namely burying the fragments of the stela in a safe place. All the boys had returned to the beach south of Castillo when Gann, John, and I joined Muddy at the bight. We dug a hole in the sand and carried the five recovered fragments thither, laid them down, and covered them again with sand. John cut a rude cross on a rock on the southern side of the bight. From this cross it is two paces north to the first stone and then three paces inland will uncover the other four. This seemed quite like Treasure Island.

We returned by way of the Castillo, where I had left my Kodak, and in passing by Temple 7 I thought to stop within to see whether we could have missed any fragments of the monument. As I stepped up on the terrace in front of the temple, I stumbled on a stone, which to my amazement had glyphs on it. It was indeed a part of the stela which we had failed to find earlier, chiefly because we had only looked inside the temple. It was probably one of those fragments carried outside by Howe and Parmelee in 1911 but not removed to the beach by them. At first I thought it was the missing fragment of the Initial Series, that showing the day 8 *Ahau*, but I soon discovered it was the last two glyphs in the same column, in fact the lower left hand corner of the sculptured part of the front of the monument.

Happily these two glyphs were unusually clear for this monument and unmistakably record a lahuntun ending on the day 7 *Ahau*. Thus it confirmed in no uncertain fashion the results obtained yesterday afternoon from a study of the other side of the monument.

Here immediately following the Initial Series we have declared a lahuntun ending 7 *Ahau*, but when was there such a lahuntun? The first occurrence of one before the Initial Series date was in 9.0.10.0.0 [A.D. 445] 6 katuns earlier, and the first occurrence after was in 9.13.10.0.0 [A.D. 702] 7 katuns later, neither of which develops any significant relation with the Initial Series itself, but if we chose the second lahuntun after the Initial Series ending on the day 7*Ahau*, we develop a higher significant relation with the Initial Series —none other than that of being exactly 1 cycle later, namely 10.6.10.0.0 [A.D. 958].

This discovery Gann and I regarded as strongly corroborating our hypothesis of yesterday, and we were correspondingly elated. It delayed us about three quarters of an hour, as I had to draw both glyphs to scale and photograph them. Just as I finished this job, Gann kicked over another smaller stone on the same terrace which proved to be another fragment of the same monument. I was able to tell that this came from the right hand side of the front near the bottom, but contained only one complete glyph and that undecipherable. It was a normal type head. It is probable that if we could have lingered longer, we might have found another piece or so. We had recovered enough, however, to encourage us to believe that possibly we may soon clear up the mystery of the most perplexing but highly important monument.

The boys were waiting at the beach to take us off. Gann and John feared a drenching and undressed to the skin, took off everything in fact except their hats. I snapped them while they were all in the surf, carrying their clothes high above their heads out to the jolly boat.

I had George carry me out on his shoulders, and I made the jolly boat without getting wet. At once we put out to the Lilian Y. As soon as we were aboard, we had breakfast and started northward for Puerto Morales.

1920

SEARCH FOR XULTÚN

Four years after the discovery of Uaxactún (where the Baktun 8 Initial Series date had been found) Morley was led to another nearby previously unknown city, which he named Xultún. The importance of this site to Morley was that he read one inscription as A.D. 889, at that time the most recent date by some twenty years of any recorded on Classic stelae. It was learned later that that same year was commemorated on at least two other southern lowland stelae—one at Uaxactún discovered in 1922 and one at Xamantun (La Muñeca) discovered in 1934—but A.D. 889 (10.3.0.0.0) does appear near the terminal date for period marking stelae erected by the Petén Maya.

Xultún, located on high ground between the Ixcan and Uaxactún valleys northeast of the site of Uaxactún, was discovered in 1915 by a chiclero named Aurelio Aguayo. Morley, guided by Aurelio, led the first archaeological party there for three days in May, 1920, and returned briefly the following season. These expeditions found Xultún to have been an extensive settlement, perhaps the largest in northeast Petén, composed of two principal plazas with some seventeen major buildings, twenty-two sculptured stelae, and as many as fifty outlying plazas. When encountered, Stela 10, which bears the late date, was found broken into three pieces and scattered on the middle of the old stairway leading to the most imposing temple in the largest group, in 1920 still partially roofed. The range of dates ultimately recorded reveal the site to have been occupied for approximately three hundred fifty years, with a beginning about midway in the early Classic period but an active populace in residence after other cities to the south apparently had been abandoned or at least had ceased the practice of stela erection.

The settlement's location in the north central Petén and its population lingering toward the end of the ninth century led Morley to suggest its potential importance in a tenth century influence upon the Río Bec region of Yucatán, but as previously mentioned, his theory of Yucatán having been colonized by people migrating out of the Petén about A.D. 900, or at the end of the Classic period, is no longer acceptable to most students of the Maya.

For four seasons after the rebel attack on his party and the resulting death of Lafleur, Morley had stayed out of the Petén. But finally in 1920 he and a young archaeologist friend, Carl Guthe, went into the remote capital town of Flores to see if any chicleros had brought in news of more unexplored ruins in the bush. No one knew of new ruins, but the two scientists spent some time exploring the site of Tayasal on Lake Petén Itzá, the point to which the Itzá were thought to have retreated after they left Yucatán in the fifteenth century. Before departing for Benque Viejo in British Honduras, Guthe made plans for excavation of this site later in the season.

Once at Benque Viejo news of a possible discovery led them back into the jungle on the trek which is recounted below.

May 21, Friday

We were up before 5:00 and almost had an early start except that a mule got bogged in the mud at the side of the aguada. This delayed us for half an hour.

It was decided that Carl, Chico, and I should push on in to Benque Viejo today, but that the mulada should sleep tonight at Santa Cruz and come into Benque tomorrow. With this understanding, we moved ahead, making excellent time by covering the eleven leagues between Ixtinta and Benque in nine hours. We had been on the road from Flores to Benque just forty-seven hours, having left Flores at 4:15 Wednesday afternoon.

This really long day did not begin to drag until after we had left Sayab. The mules were about done up and we also. It was not until the last league when they began to recognize some of their surroundings that they came to life. Fortunately, it was not a very hot day, though we grew thirsty before the end. We stopped at Yaxha only long enough for me to find out that the alcalde had gone to his milpa. I had wanted to ask him about ruins north of Yaxha.

On this Flores-Benque highway sooner or later one meets every muleteer one has ever known. Yesterday, for example, at Culek we picked up a boy who had been my muleteer to Ucanal, down by Smith's mahogany camp on the Mopan River, in 1914. He remembered me and I, him; we talked over that trip. Today just beyond Santa Cruz I met a man who was at Laguna de Yaloch when Carpenter, Lafleur, and I passed through there in May, 1916, enroute to Uaxactún. Lafleur treated this man for some illness. The fellow told me that when he heard of the doctor's death, he cried. It seemed to me a strange coincidence that we should thus be thrown together for a moment on the Flores-Benque highway. I shook his hand, and we parted.

Up to this point we passed several muladas, those which had left Sayab that morning, but from now on to Gavilán we met none. We stopped at Gavilán for twenty minutes for a light lunch of tea, biscuits, Spanish sausage, Horlick's malted milk tablets, and a tin of pears. It was as dry as a dry smoke, though the pears helped.

We got away from Gavilán at twenty minutes before 12:00 and soon began to meet patachos which had set out from Plancha de Piedra that morning.
I know the distance between Gavilán and Sayab to be two leagues, but as we
passed one long patacho, I asked each man the distance from Sayab. The
answers as I got them were: two leagues, three leagues, one league, and four
leagues. This was an interesting commentary on the veracity and judgment of
these arrieros when it comes to estimating distances.

This section of the day's run we covered in good time, doing the two
leagues between Sayab and Plancha in one hour and forty minutes. At Plancha we paid our respects to Don Pablo. I asked him in passing what he had
found out about the new ruin. He told me the guide was in Yaloch, an easy
lie.

We went next to the place where iced drinks could be had, a cantina
belonging to Domingo Espat, and had some ginger ale. It was not imported,
but I have never tasted anything sweeter. Then we walked up the hill to the
padre's.

We had not been at the padre's for half an hour when a nice looking
Petenero came up the hill with a story of a ruin three days north of El Cayo
which he claimed contains five or six stelae sculptured with hieroglyphics. It
sounded too good to be true. I suspected at once that it could only be La
Honradez. It was in the same direction from El Cayo as La Honradez, though
it did not seem so far off, and had about the same number of stelae. I talked
with this boy for upwards of an hour, trying in every way to ascertain
whether it could be La Honradez or not. He naturally feels that it is not, as
indeed I hope. But after the El Sos fiasco, I am shy of another long trip only
to see something I already know. I told him that tomorrow my baggage
would be here, and I had notes in it which I thought might solve the question. He will return tomorrow.

May 22, Saturday

Spent the greater part of the day talking to Sixto Cambranes and
Aurelio Aguayo. Sixto is supposed to be the best chiclero of either Cayo or
Benque, which means that he knows this northeastern Petén bush better
than anyone else. I asked him to give me a complete list of places where there
were sculptured monuments. He gave me four names as follows: Tikal, Bam-
bonal (Uaxactún), Invierno (Naranjo), and Taliche. I had seen all but the
last, and this after much questioning, he weakened on at last and said he was
not sure whether it had figures or not but that Aurelio would remember.

When I first heard of this stela, I said we would go there Monday. It is
not far beyond the Río Holmul and stands right by one of the roads leading
into the interior. But later when Sixto weakened, and especially when Aurelio
said he could not remember if it was carved or not, I gave up the idea. I told
Sixto he could verify the matter this season. If it is carved, he can take me to
it when I return next March. I have strong doubts about it because Aurelio

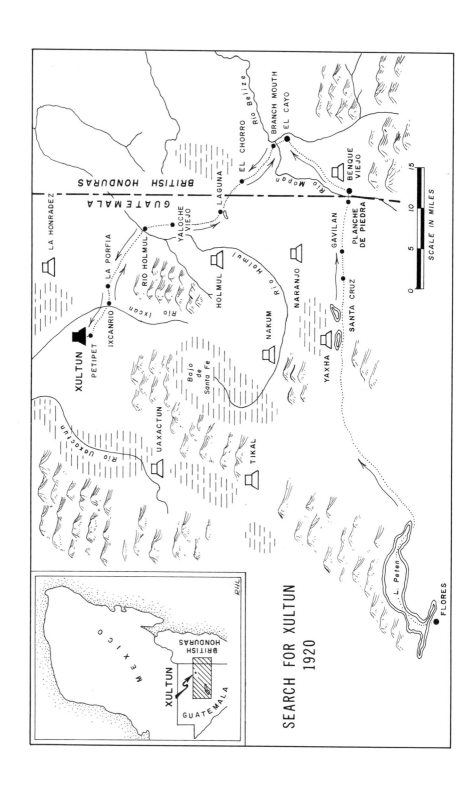

SEARCH FOR XULTUN
1920

says the American who worked at Holmul (Merwin and his brother) cleaned and photographed it. If this is so, it must have been a plain stela, otherwise Merwin would have mentioned it to me.

For some time now I have had an idea, which Father Versavel helped me to carry out, of having some placards printed in Spanish as an announcement to the chicleros of Benque Viejo and El Cayo that when they go to the bush to bleed chicle on their next trip, they mark any places in the bush "ruinas antiguas" where there are carved or sculptured stones with either figures or letters. Furthermore, that on my return next March, I will pay any individual who guides me to a place of this description and shows me the monument the sum of twenty-five dollars gold for every new place. Interested chicleros are to communicate such discoveries to Father Versavel at Benque or Edward Enright at El Cayo. Father Versavel helped me put this "aviso" into Spanish. When I return to Belize, I am going to have it printed at the Clarion Press and will then send the placards up to Benque and Cayo to be put around in the various stores and cantinas. Both Cambranes and Aguayo think it will bring in many notices of such discoveries. When I return in March, I hope to reap the harvest.

About 3:00 in the afternoon Eulogio, Michael, and Rosa got in. As soon as I could get into my kyack, I got out my La Honradez notes and tried to ascertain from them whether Aurelio's site could be the same one or not. But even after making the map of La Honradez and locating the stelae on it, I could not feel sure. Aurelio, on the contrary, feels confident that it is a new site and bases his belief on a very strong point. Percy Adams and I were at La Honradez at the end of February, 1915. While there, I had a well defined trail cleared into the ruins and the trees and underbrush around each stela cut down. Aurelio was at his site only seven months later, in September and October, 1915. He says he found *no sign of any sort* of a previous visitor. It is impossible that clearings made no more than six or seven months before his visit would not have been apparent to a skilled bushman. The obvious conclusion is that the two are not the same site, which I earnestly hope is the case. His site, he stoutly avers, has nine or ten monuments.

I have decided to take him over to El Cayo with me tomorrow and lay the whole matter before Natalio Guzmán, because he is about the only one left who remembers where old Eleuterio Fernández had his first jato ten years ago, which was within a mile of the ruins of La Honradez. If Natalio Guzmán thinks they are different places, I am willing to chance it, although it means a hard bush trip of at least a week. Aurelio's place is three good jornadas northwest of Cayo.

With this plan, I dismissed Aurelio for the day. We will take him to Cayo with us in the automobile in the morning. If Natalio reports favorably, we will start for the ruins the next day.

May 24, Monday

At last at 9:25 we were ready to start. The Mopan River is now so low that it can be forded just above Branch Mouth, to which ford we were now going. The water was not deep, and we got over without difficulty.

Beyond, Miguel took a short cut which went through a second growth thicket. Here we all had to turn arriero and urge the mules forward. They had little desire to do this and kept stopping every little bit and looking back. By dint of much profanity and beating, we finally got them through the thicket and on to the main trail.

After winding through the thickly overgrown valley plain of the Belize River, we entered a very narrow stony bottomed arroyo and commenced to ascend it. It had rained while we were crossing the valley, and the rocks were slippery. One of the cargo animals slipped on a smooth slab, went down, and almost stood on its head. I felt sure it had broken its neck. Miguel hurried forward and gave it a push; it staggered to its feet and leisured on, apparently none the worse. After getting out of the arroyo, we stopped a minute for the boys to adjust the packs. My animal improved the occasion by lying down with me on his back. I lost no time in helping him to his feet, however, with every means at my disposal.

After winding over quite a little range, always amid dense vegetation, we descended. At the bottom of the hill we reached El Chorro, four and three quarters hours out.

We stopped here to arrange the packs. A group of mounds extend back from the champas. The area is cleared, and is quite cheerful. In the little plaza of the mounds to which Carl wandered to explore he found a cache of clothes and cooking utensils.

We left El Chorro at 2:30 and reached Laguna at 5:25. The last time I had ridden into this little settlement was under very different circumstances as Lafleur, Carpenter, and I were getting under way on our 1916 trip which was to end so tragically.

This time it was very different. The houses were all gone save one, burned by Trinidad Flores's motley crew when they finally fled north from Laguna toward Mexico. There were two galleries, a large one which was already occupied, and a small one, which we took. The owner of the mulada already camped was that of Don Antonio Maldonado of El Cayo, a Campeche citizen by birth and an old friend. We exchanged greetings, and he insisted upon our taking some food until our dinner should be ready.

We had supper about dusk and turned in early. In the night Chico was so troubled with mosquitoes that he abandoned his hammock and slept on the ground under Aurelio's pabellon.

May 25, Tuesday

The boys were up before daylight, and in consequence we got a fairly early start. Antonio Maldonado had advised us to go by way of La Cubeta, where he said there was plenty of good water. The water at La Porfia was re-ported to be nothing but mud. In spite of this advice, both Aurelio and Miguel were in favor of going to La Porfia because it was much shorter for us. We skirted around the northern end of the lake, and then headed almost due northwest. Indeed for the seven and a half hours we were traveling today, we maintained this general direction.

At one and three quarters hours out, the trail forks. The left hand branch goes to Triumfo, being that we followed four years ago on our way to Uaxactún. The right branch is the one we followed this morning to La Porfia. Three hours from Laguna we passed Yaloch Viejo. If I am not mistaken, it was here in a chultun that that beautiful cache of pottery was found many years ago. Gann acquired half the cache and Davis half. I think now it is all in the Heye Museum in New York. [See Gann, 1918, pl. 23-28]

After this, for the next hour we passed mound after mound. Four hours and a half out we entered the bajo of the Río Holmul and were in it for half an hour. These bajos are bottom lands usually along watercourses which in the rainy season are nothing more than logwood swamps. Branches hang very low, and the pack animals are continually becoming entangled. We had to watch constantly to avoid ugly blows from low bejucos. Several times our hats were swept off.

After leaving the bajo of the Río Holmul, we commenced ascending a high range on the north side of the Holmul valley. This range really is the divide between the Belize and the Holmul Rivers. The river we will cross tomorrow, the Ixcanrio, flows into the Hondo. It is a fairly high range for Petén, and took us a long time to get over it.

We reached La Porfia at 3:00. Miguel went to the aguada at once and re-ported fair water. The two galerones were in good condition. We housed ourselves comfortably for the night. We left the lantern burning to ward off the chance visit of a tigre, which is not a true tiger but the American jaguar.

May 26, Wednesday

It was a dry night. The rains are still holding off, and luck is with us in that respect at least. In spite of an early rising, Aurelio and Miguel were late getting the mules. When they finally brought the latter back, they ate a lengthy breakfast with the result that, although we were up a half hour earlier than yesterday, before they had loaded the mules and we were ready to start, it was 7:30.

Today's journey led across the valley plain of the Ixcanrio. The first hour and three-quarters of the day from La Porfia to the crossing of the Ixcanrio we pursued the same general direction as yesterday, namely due northwest. The next three and a half hours after leaving the Ixcanrio, the direction changed to half way between west and northwest and so continued to our journey's end, the champas of Petipet, Maya for "two brothers."

Earlier after leaving Ixcanrio we had begun to pass through a group of mounds, two at first, and later quite a number. These continued for three-quarters of an hour. We judged it to be a fairly important group. Some of the mounds were high enough to be called pyramids. We felt a search might disclose stelae. Just after passing this group, I asked Aurelio how far his ruins lay from where we now were. He said we had just passed his old blaze of five years ago, and that the monuments lay no more than a shout to the north of the trail. It was evident then that the mounds through which we had just been passing were all part of his city, the outlying plazas possibly to the south.

Although he was tired because the mules had been particularly obnoxious all day long—eating zapotes when we wanted them to go forward and rushing at every low hanging bough they saw with the hope of scraping us off—I prevailed upon him to go back, look up the ruins, and make himself sure of the monuments. Very obligingly he did this while we continued on to Petipet, which we reached thirty-six minutes after passing the last mound of the above group.

At Petipet there were a number of small shallow pools filled with water the color of strong tea and covered with algae. The champas were not half bad, though we picked the worst one at first. Not until after we had unloaded did we discover better ones to which we moved at once.

After four Aurelio returned dripping with perspiration and tired out but bringing the welcome news that he had succeeded in finding the ruins and that there were three standing monuments and three fallen ones. The ruins were not more than a half mile north of the group of mounds we had passed.

I calculated his blaze to be about two and a half miles back along the trail. That plus another half mile to the monuments made three miles we would have to cover from camp to the scene of our labors and back, a total of six miles daily. This meant carrying lunch with us.

We had a good supper and retired early against the prospects of a busy exciting day tomorrow. I could not get to sleep at once for thinking of what we might find in the way of new dates.

May 27, Thursday

We were all up early in anticipation of an early start for the ruins. The walk back over the trail was laborious. Most of it was through a low swamp, the trail much cut up by the mules and now hardened into hummocks which made walking a chore. It took us thirty-eight minutes to reach the last mound we passed yesterday afternoon, and then sixteen minutes more to reach the blaze where Aurelio's picado came in. From there it was just twenty-two minutes walk north and east through the bush to the principal plaza. The ruins seem to be about due east of the parage of Petipet.

Before reaching the principal plaza, we passed eight subsidiary plazas and several chultunes. We passed a high house on our left, or on the west side of the Great Plaza, and came to the first stela. This was fairly well executed, but appeared to me to be only half its original height; that is, the figure entered the ground at its waist. There were no glyphs on it. Stela 2 stood next it, and while complete, was unfortunately badly eroded. There were no glyphs on the back and sides so far as I could tell. The two vertical panels on the front appeared to have no calendrical signs.

Stela 3 stood in front of Structure 11. It was broken in half, the lower part still being in situ. In addition to this, it had split along the narrow sides so that the front half was practically complete. The part of the base in situ was only the back half of the monument. The front half of the bottom half we raised later. There had been glyphs on the sides of this stela, but I could do nothing with them.

Stela 4 was standing. Although the sides had glyphs, they were so far gone that I could do nothing with them either.

Stela 5 had broken near the ground, and the monument had fallen forward face down in one great piece. The glyphs on one side of this were very clear. Unfortunately they were of unknown meaning.

Stela 7 had fallen forward on its face; faint traces of glyph columns, two on each narrow face appeared, but I could not decipher them. Stelae 8 and 9 had both fallen forward on their faces. In each case fairly large trees were growing on top of them, with roots thrown down over the sides of the stones and clasping them in a grip which had actually cracked and even crumbled them. Carl found Stela 6. It is small, low, and built in so close to the sub-structures of structure IV that it is almost completely buried. It has one curious and very unusual feature: the glyphs are intaglio.

The preliminary inspection of the nine monuments discovered proved very discouraging since it looked as though we were not going to get a single date.

We next climbed the high structure I, the loftiest building at the site, the summit of which towers above the highest vegetation on the plain below. Its ground plan was simple of the so-called temple type with outer chamber and an inner sanctuary. The view from the top of the roof comb was splendid. When we finally oriented ourselves with the compass, we saw stretching across the horizon far off to the southeast and cutting the view in that direction a high range. Between this high ridge and ourselves stretched a great rolling plain covered with the dense forest through which we passed yesterday. From our lofty lookout it appeared to be a carpet of green, which on closer inspection broke down into individual clumps of trees, succeeding low ridges which did not rise above the distant range to the south, and spots of varying color.

We were now hot, tired, thirsty, and disappointed. We descended the temple pyramid to eat lunch on the round altar of Stela 1. It was a meagerish lunch of tea biscuit, jam, chipped beef, veal loaf, and a tin of apricots. This dry repast was washed down with a bottle of Benque Viejo soda pop, whose chief merit lay in the fact that it was moist.

While we were eating, a troop of perhaps fifteen monkeys came through the tree tops, chattering and growling. Chico was fired with the ambition to kill one instantly and loudly lamented the fact that he had not brought the old shotgun he had found at Ixcanrio. He threw many stones. The monkeys became enraged and shook the branches. Broken boughs fell and a mild excitement reigned. The monkeys retired to a corner of the plaza and continued to shout their defiance from time to time. After lunch Chico and Aurelio climbed the substructure of Temple VI and hurled stones down on them from above.

Chico and Aurelio, in cruising along the eastern edge of the substructure of Temple VI, found a stela (No. 12) fallen face forward, broken into three pieces. We cleaned off the vegetable mold, fallen leaves, decomposed stone, and earth, and turned the top part first. The upper half of a beautifully executed human figure rewarded these efforts. On the next fragment to the left in front of the figure was a column of four glyphs, beginning with a Calendar Round date and a Secondary Series, which filled the last three blocks. What delighted us particularly was the extraordinary state of preservation of the carving.

We next directed our attention to the bottom fragment which was more deeply buried. This required more excavation, and our only tools were two machetes. Finally the earth and roots were cleared from its edges, and we turned it over. It was the bottom half of our priest and was as well preserved as the top part.

Next we jimmied these three pieces into their proper relative positions and gave the face a good scrubbing with a stiff bristled brush I had brought for the purpose, and the whole design was revealed.

A priest facing to the left held in his right hand, extended before his face, a beautiful little tiger figure seated upon its haunches. It was so well preserved at this point that even the delicate lining on the spots of the body still showed clearly. From this little feline's mouth there issued a scroll, which rose above its head terminating in a graceful flower which resembled a conventionalized lily. A small companion figure was seated on the elbow of the left arm of the priest, this figure had a death head. The details of the priest's costume were elaborate, not to say gorgeous, and the large headdress in which feathers played a conspicuous part was sumptuous. Our work made Stela 10 ready for photographing, and we scattered to other work.

Carl called my attention to an interesting stucco decoration on the roof comb of Temple II. We climbed the pyramid to study this closer and were intent upon its examination when a heavy shower came up. We hastily took shelter in what was left of the temple itself, a small section in front of the sanctuary. Presently the rain fell so heavily that it began to drop in tiny streams from many places. Carl conceived the happy idea of arranging our mouths under some of these. This was rain water and therefore to be trusted. I selected a promising infant Niagara and, turning up my face, allowed the tiny thread of delicious cool refreshing water to trickle down my throat. In

Typical forest of northern Petén. Species of *Sabal* and *Ficus* in foreground. Photographed near Uaxactún by O. F. Cook. All plates in this section originally appeared in publications of the Carnegie Institute of Washington.

An *aguada* near Uaxactún. The floating plant is *Pistia stratiotes (lechuga)*. The tree around the edges is *pachira aguatica (zapotebobo)*. Photographed by O.F. Cook.

ght: Uaxactún expedition on road
~shly cut through logwood swamp.

low: Freighting by launch on the
lize River. This is El Cayo landing
itish Honduras.

Above: Pack train of the Uaxactún expedition. *Below:* The 1916 campsite at Uaxactún.

Above: Stela 6 at Uaxactún, front view.

Right: Stela 9 (8.14.10.13.15) at Uaxactún. For many years this was the
oldest known Maya stela.

View at Tuluum on the Caribbean, looking south from temple 45.

Looking north from the Castillo at Tuluum. Photographs by Samuel Lothrop.

Left: Tuluum Stela 1 (9.6.10.0.0). *Right*: Xultún Stela 18. Scale is approximately 1/20.

Stela 3 (10.1.10.0.0) and Stela 1 (10.3.0.0.0) at Xultún. Scale is approximately 1/20 .

Above: Usumacinta River at Piedras Negras, looking north. Sacrificial rock is on river bank at left. *Below:* Piedras Negras expedition campsite in 1921.

(a)   (b)   (c)

Piedras Negras. Stela 37, left and right side views (a and b). Stela 39, left side (c).

Three views of Stela 40 at Piedras Negras.

Left and right sides of Stela 12 at Piedras Negras.

Above: Campsite at Calakmul, amid grove of ramon trees (ramonal). *Below:* Another view of Calakmul, with standing stelae. Photographs by Sylvanus G. Morley.

Stela 51 (9.15.0.0.0) at Calakmul. Scale is approximately 1/20.

Top: The Calakmul expedition used this platform car, drawn by two mules in tandem, to carry personnel and baggage more than 50 miles into the interior. Normally, the cars haul blocks of chicle (crude chewing gum).

Center: La Gloria, Campeche, on the route traversed by the Calakmul expedition. At this point change was made from the platform cars to a five ton truck, which carried the party through the rain forest to within a few miles of the site.

Right: a *chiclero* tapping the *zapote* for chicle. In northern Peten, some of these trees reach a diameter of 3 feet and a height of over 100 feet.

Top: Three sculptured stelae at Calakmul. A wild fig tree grows on top of the monument at right, the roots covering the front.

Center: Stelae 28 and 29, the oldest monuments at Calakmul. Both indicate the same date, 9.9.10.0.0 in the Maya chronology, or 364 A.D.

Right: Date glyphs on the beautifully carved Stela 89 at Calakmul.

this way for many moments we partially assuaged our thirst. Indeed my first intimation that the shower was passing was the thinning and occasional interruption of my particular streamlet. Before long the blue skies broke through the blanket of clouds.

When we descended the pyramid, I found my note paper and sun helmet a sorry wreck. The latter weighed at least five pounds and was soft and squashy.

We returned to Stela 10. The sun broke through, making a fine light for photography. I took six exposures of the monument.

We now prepared to go. The boys had arranged a canvas pack cover so that it would catch rain water. They had three bottles filled which we were still thirsty enough to want. The camera and lunch containers were packed, and we started back to camp a little before 4:00. In leaving the plaza we frightened a perdis, a partridge, which flew up into the air. Under a shrub Aurelio found its nest containing seven eggs about the size of a hen's egg and of a pinkish color. Fearing these had young within, and none caring to discourage the little mother, we did not even touch them, but continued on toward camp.

If the way was weary coming out, it was certainly wearier going back, particularly the last half. This part crosses a bajo, the mud of which had dried into hummocks. Long continued hopping from one to another of these ridges — tires and bruises the instep. We reached Petipet a little after 5:00, being one hour and a quarter on the way back.

I undressed to the skin immediately after getting there to prevent ticks from transfering themselves from my clothes to my person. To my utmost dismay, on my left foot in the center of the instep I found a small black cup-shaped hole about one-tenth of an inch in diameter. It neither pained, burned, nor itched, but there it was, and I couldn't explain it. As always in this bush, I think of a snake bite first, but the boys declared that snake bites swelled and pained horribly from the first. What dread unknown malady of the bush was it? Anxiety as to its nature far transcended any incovenience from the malady itself, and I was half sick with worry over what it might or might not be. I continued the examination of my body and to my horror found another of these black cups on my left heel and three on the calf of my right leg. And then the rational explanation occurred to me, worry ceased, and I composed myself.

This morning before dressing a package of potassium permanganate had spilled on my cot. Several crystals of this had gotten under my left sock. As the day wore on and I perspired more and more, these had slowly dissolved. The close fitting puttee I wore had held them tightly in one place. Each of them had slowly eaten into the flesh below it, causing these little black cup-like depressions.

We turned in early. I was very much discouraged. This long, expensive, laborious trip, and no dates were disheartening.

May 28, Friday

It was decided this morning to take Miguel back with us to help try to lift Stela 5 and also to cut down the tree above Stela 8. When we were ready to set off, he was absent at the ramonal. We left a note in camp for him to follow with the ax as soon as he could.

We set out for the ruins. At the point where Aurelio's picado branches off, I left my handkerchief on a sapling as a sign for him to follow.

As soon as we arrived at the ruins, the four of us freed the upper half of Stela 3 from its blanket of humus, roots, leaves, and broken rotten stone and turned it over. The upper part of the priestly figure there preserved was very like that on Stela 10, holding the same little tiger in its right palm. It was in practically as good condition as Stela 10. We jimmied the two pieces together for photographing.

Meanwhile as Miguel had not yet arrived, it was useless to attempt to raise Stela 5. Carl returned to his mapping, while I began to draw the glyph panels on the front of Stelae 3 and 10. Aurelio set off into the bush. Some time later we heard distant calls and gave answering halloos. Presently Miguel, with an ax arrived. As Aurelio was now missing, I put Miguel to cutting the roots of the tree on top of Stela 8. My idea was that if the roots were severed at the ground level, the tree would fall, turning over with it the monument grasped in its roots.

While Miguel attacked this problem, I returned to my drawing, but after a while the cutting ceased. So I sent Chico to ascertain why. It seems that although all the roots were cut, the tree would not fall, I believed this due in part to the engagement of its upper branches with the branches of a neighboring tree and in part to the heavy weight of the stela itself which prevented the tree from falling, in spite of the fact that it had a decided cant to the northwest.

A big bejuco hung on the side. We tried pulling on this but to no purpose. Finally I gave it up as a bad job. Shortly, however, Aurelio came back, and calling Carl from his mapping, we all tried to turn Stela 5. The heavy mass of this fragment proved too much for us. After getting the edge we were lifting a foot and a half off the ground, we had to abandon the project.

By this time we were all hungry and tired and by common consent adjourned to the lunch table, the altar of Stela 1. No monkeys called on us this noon.

Afterwards we scattered to our work, Carl back to his mapping; Miguel back to Petipet, Chico, Aurelio, and I back to Stela 10, where I wanted to take a final photograph and then throw it back on its face to protect it from the rain. Also I wanted to have a last try at its right edge in hopes that I might find an Initial Series there. Aurelio and Carl were not inclined to view with enthusiasm the overthrowing of the monument on which we had expended so much time, but finally we put it back face down.

I took my scrubbing brush and rubbed up the glyphs on the right side.

Only the left edges of these were preserved. At first I saw nothing but two bars fifteen and a half inches long. For a moment I thought these must be parts of some decorative side panel like one of the stelae at Piedras Negras, but suddenly it struck me that this was the two bars of a Cycle 10 Initial Series. Just above it where my eye fell next was the curve of the tun element of the Initial Series Introducing Glyph. At this point I shouted excitedly, "Carl – a Cycle 10 Initial Series."

In any Maya date the most important coefficient is always that of the katun sign, so my eye hurriedly followed down to this. Here came the greatest surprise and most amazing discovery of the entire trip. It was 3, making this monument the latest known in the Old Maya Empire. This I fairly roared to Carl, "The latest Initial Series known in the whole Old Empire!" I heard a great crashing as Carl came hurtling through the bush in an equal frenzy of excitement. I had already found the 0 tuns and by the time he arrived, was able to give him the final reading as 10.3.0.0.0 1 *Ahau*, 3 *Yaxkin*, about A.D. 889 and twenty years later than the latest previously discovered stelae from the Old Empire: Stela 2 at Flores, Stela 1 at Seibal, and Stela 11 at Tikal.

It was a great discovery and immediately changed our plans. We had been planning on finishing this afternoon and leaving tomorrow for La Porfia. But now that I would have to draw this, it would make me stay over another day. Carl was glad of this, as he said it would enable him to do a better job on the map.

This discovery at once raised the hope that a similar Initial Series might yet be found on Stela 3, whither we immediately removed ourselves and threw it also over on its face. I was kneeling down by its right side almost before it fell and in another second was reading the following important and never found before Initial Series 10.1.10.0.0 4 *Ahau* 13 *Kankin* [A.D. 859]. It was almost too good to be true. Two Cycle 10 Initial Series and only three others are known anywhere else and both new, and one, the latest date in the Old Empire.

We were both greatly excited. I could scarcely compose myself sufficiently to draw. Finally I settled down, however, to the Initial Series of Stela 3 and finished the four glyph blocks on the right side—Initial Series introducing glyph, cycles, katuns, and tuns—in what remained of a very eventful afternoon filled with one of the most important discoveries of my field career.

And now I must take up another matter which may prove of importance. In his cruising through the bush, this morning Aurelio came on another plaza filled with seven sculptured monuments. This plaza was about a kilometer to the northeast. He told me of this in the afternoon but said he was saving it to show me the next year.

I saw at once what was troubling him. It was so near the site we are now working on that he feared I would regard it as the same and not give him an extra twenty-five dollars for it unless he held it over until next year. Of course, if it is only a kilometer distant, it is technically and actually part of the same site. But I saw that if I were to see it all this year, I must regard it as a new site. I therefore told him that if it were that far distant from the first group, I would regard it as a new site and give him an extra twenty-five dollars for leading me to it in the morning.

On the way home, tired as we were, we speculated on the new dates and the effect of their news upon our friends of the Maya society. I can just imagine old Gann's eyes fairly popping out of his head. We talked of what we should name the site. This latest date of all suggested the propriety of incorporating in whatever Maya name we choose the Maya word Xul, which means "end" or "close." Carl thought a one syllable word not so desirable as a two syllable one. I thought Xul might be confused with the modern village of Xul in Yucatán, where Stephens also speaks of archaeological remains. We reached home before half past five, and while Carl was supervising the preparation of dinner, I succeeded in tying in the two Calendar Round dates and Secondary Series to the respective Initial Series on Stelae 3 and 10.

It has been a very eventful day. These two discoveries alone have put an entirely new aspect on our entire trip, which up to the point of this afternoon's discovery, I had been disposed to regard in the light of a failure. Now, however, we can bring home new dates, and important ones too.

The afternoon's discoveries show that this site must have been one of the very latest, if not *the* latest Old Empire city to be occupied, and indeed has increased the period of the Old Empire by another twenty years. Finally, it shows that this site was occupied for at least ten years after the single Initial Series yet found at Chichén Itzá, namely 10.2.10.0.0 [A.D. 879].

May 29, Saturday

We got off at quarter to seven and covered the first half of the route to the ruins in good time. We stopped at the ruins only long enough to leave the lunch and then going to the northeast corner of the plaza, we struck due northeast, crossing several mounds and a small quarry. Here we found what I have never seen before, a half finished stela which seems to have broken in ancient times. This is well squared but only about four feet high. The top is broken. After another five minutes' walk, we came to a plaza with a small stela standing in it. This later was to receive the number 11. It was sculptured on the front with a figure and glyphs on the sides. These, like those on Stela 6 at Group A, are intaglio.

Aurelio next led us to a fine standing monument. It is some seven or eight feet high. So far as I could detect, it was sculptured only on the front with a large figure facing most unusually to the right. Another equally unusual feature was the absence of any glyphs on it, which I think is almost unique. This stela was later given the number 12.

Aurelio next led us to four very large stelae which had all fallen forward and which had all been quite tall, standing at least ten feet above ground. One was caught in the roots of a large tree which grew on top of it. Burrowing down along the right side of this, I detected traces of an Initial Series and think I read this as 9.15.0.0.0 4 *Ahau* 13 *Yax* [A.D. 731], although this is doubtful. Another stela in the group also had an Initial Series on its right side, but the details of the glyphs are so deteriorated that I could not even hazard a guess as to the date recorded here.

Stela 15, however, provided a certain date. On the left side the fourth glyph down I noticed was Glyph A of the Supplementary Series. The following glyph was very clearly 13 *Muan* and the next, end of katun 14. The first, second, and third glyphs I next succeeded in deciphering as Glyphs C, X, and B of the Supplementary Series. It became evident that the ten or eleven glyphs on the right side, now unfortunately practically entirely eroded, had recorded the following Initial Series number, the day of the terminal date and the first three or four glyphs of the Supplementary Series. The date recorded here was therefore 9.14.0.0.0 6 *Ahau* 13 *Muan,* end of Katun 14 [A.D. 711].

This date, toward the close of the Middle Period, to 10.3.0.0.0 [A.D. 889] shows a recorded occupation of one hundred eighty years.

The discovery of this second place shows that this site was fairly extensive, at least a third class city and possibly a second class one.

The plaza discovered this morning was older than the Great Plaza of Group A and although the monuments are higher at the former, they are not so highly developed stylistically.

Stela 14 is so badly eroded that I could not even tell whether there had ever been glyphs on its sides. Since the other three associated ones are in the same line and had Initial Series, I believe this had formerly had one also. These four stelae had all fallen face forward, and the sculptures on these faces should be in excellent states of preservation.

Aurelio reported to me later that there is one other stela fallen and broken, to which I gave the number 18. This makes eight sculptured monuments for this Group B, which, added to the ten already found at Group A, makes eighteen for the entire ruin.

There are five stelae that will have to be turned here at Group B, and four at Group A. If these yield us fine figures on their faces, it will make a spectacular series of sculptures and well worth returning here to turn them over. If they all carry Calendar Round dates and Secondary Series on their fronts, even if the Initial Series on their sides are effaced, I think I can probably date them. At any rate we now have at least six new Initial Series, of which three have been read surely and one doubtfully.

In the meantime, Carl had returned to Group A, while I remained behind to take such notes as might be necessary at Group B. I finished here about 11:00 and returned with Chico and Aurelio to the other group.

As it was an hour yet until noon and I wanted to finish Stela 3 before drawing the Initial Series on Stela 10, I worked here first, and then adjourned to Stela 10, where we all ate lunch. Afterward I drew the Initial Series on Stela 10. Then after a last photograph or two, I was ready to go.

Carl in the meantime had worked around the great plaza and was finishing the last structure, Temple VI on the west side. Temple VI must have been an imposing construction; so far as we could make out, it consisted of two long parallel chambers, close on to one hundred feet in length, broken here and there by transverse walls, though not by many of them. Traces of a roof comb with niches in it were observed at the southern end. From the floor of the chamber to the capstone of this arch must have been all of fifteen feet.

Carl finished about 3:00, and after gathering our effects together, taking a last look at the Great Plaza, and bidding goodbye to the little partridge mother, we set off for Petipet with light hearts.

On the way back we decided on the name for the ancient city. I have spoken already how we both felt the propriety of having Xul in the name to commemorate or symbolize the fact that this was the last or "end" city of the Old Empire. That this fact had further been recorded on a monument here, a "stone," Maya "tun," and that such a stone was the closing stone or "end stone," suggested the name Xultún, which was the one we finally adopted for this city. The more we said this over, the better it sounded, and we came to refer quite naturally even on the way back to camp to the city of Xultún.

We reached camp at 4:30 and set about preparing to leave. I first changed clothes, celebrating our coming departure by a clean pair of riding trousers. We began to ease up somewhat on food restrictions also, because we planned to be in Cayo on Tuesday night, the first of June, Carl's twenty-sixth birthday.

The sun set fair, and a pleasant day seemed promised for tomorrow. The moonlight falling through the bush is lovely, and it literally floods the forest with its brilliance.

1921

RETURN TO PIEDRAS NEGRAS

Piedras Negras is one of three major Maya sites located in the middle Usumacinta valley in the extreme western part of the Department of Petén. Although it apparently rose to prominence several centuries after Classic Uaxactún had become a leading center and lacked an underlying Preclassic horizon, Piedras Negras, together with Palenque and Yaxchilan, produced what many persons consider the most outstanding sculptures of the pre-Hispanic New World.

A large ceremonial center located on a bluff overlooking an important river route to the interior, Piedras Negras flourished during the Classic period. It is one of only two cities which ultimately was capable of regularly erecting stelae to mark the passage not only of twenty and ten year cycles but also of five year periods. Piedras Negras thus is remarkable in that each hotun marker from A.D. 608 to A.D. 810 now has been found there, although the city has produced other stelae dates as early as A.D. 435.

Teobert Maler in 1895 was the first European to happen upon the ruins of Piedras Negras, now in Guatemala, but at that time prior to a change in the international boundary, in Mexico. He had heard of them from the foreman of their discoverer, a native of the Mexican town of Tenosique, who had found the mounds the year before as he prepared a new monteria for his mahogany operations. Maler visited the site four different times, on the last trip in 1899 staying for three months and preparing a report for the Peabody Museum of Harvard.

Morley, having been inspired by Maler's report, was eager to go to Piedras Negras and included the site in his first circuit of the Petén although it lay on the western fringe of the district and reaching it involved an arduous journey. He returned in 1921, accompanied by Oliver G. Ricketson and Arthur K. Rutherford, after an unusually strenuous trek from Flores west to La Libertad, northwest to Tenosique, Mexico, and then looping back south along the Usumacinta to the site. This expedition found five new monuments which had been overlooked in earlier surveys. Morley deciphered nine more

Initial Series dates which were found to fill in the lacunae in the sequence of hotun markers so that every 1800-day period for one hundred sixty-five years was shown to be recorded. In 1929 and 1931 he came to Piedras Negras again but remained only a few days each time.

During the 1930's, expeditions from the Museum of the University of Pennsylvania spent eight seasons at Piedras Negras. These archaeologists unearthed numerous ceremonial objects and pieces of such exquisite sculpture that the site gained fame as the home of the highest artistic achievements.

The journal passages below are taken from the 1921 diary and begin as the party is lost in the uninhabited area of western Petén.

May 5, Thursday

A bad day. We rose long before 6:00, but four mules had strayed from the corral. We had to wait about an hour to get them. I lost my spur too, which proved to be a bad omen.

We got off at 9:15 and soon were out on the open ground adjoining the river. This was the camino real to Tenosique, and the La Pita road branched off this to the left. Alfred Harvey set out with Joaquín, the captain, and his four men to clear the road, which Don Alfredo feared might be overgrown. He felt quite sure he knew the entrance for the La Pita road. This, however, was not his first trouble.

We had gone some distance down the river when we discovered that we only had fifteen cargo animals. We had started with eleven riding animals and sixteen cargo animals. We had, in addition, five men who walked. Don Alfredo was of the opinion that the missing mule had gone on before; we continued for three or four miles along the south shore of the river. He finally reached a piece of the road which showed no mule trail ahead, whereupon he advised our turning back. Before he had finally found the La Pita entrance, we had lost two hours and gone two leagues out of our way.

The missing animal was found just inside the bush on the La Pita road, the only one of the whole mulada which had gone right!

Our course lay mostly south. The road ran through a thick tangle of low bush, obviously at one time the flood plain of the river. It was very hard going. It was lucky indeed that we had sent men on to cut the road because otherwise we would have been held back. As it was, we just crept along. The mulada was collectively one of the worst I have ever seen. Individually the mules were excellent—fat, strong, and lively, too lively in fact. They darted into the bush at every opportunity and brushed off their cargoes whenever they had the opportunity.

In addition to this, poor Ricketson had his fever again.

It was about 11:00 when we finally got back on to the La Pita road. For two hours we were in low thick bottomland bush. Then the road began to rise, and at the same time, the bush grew higher. This ridge which I took to be the foothills of the range was on the south side of the San Pedro River. At

3:00 we came to the parage of La Pita. Alfred and the five boys were waiting for us here, having been in for three or four hours.

Don Alfredo said the next parage, Corozal, was three and a half leagues. It had been a bad day all around. Rick still had a fever, and we were all tired. It seemed to me to be best to stop for the day and try to make up tomorrow.

There was good water in the aguada but no champas, and worse still no ramon. The reason for this was that this place has been a parage on the camino real from La Libertad to Tenosique for more than twenty years, and the ramon nearby has been cut. This place is even on the Hedge map and approximately correctly located. This surprised me somewhat, and I was glad to have stopped at one parage on this road which I have wanted to see for a long time.

While the animals were being unloaded, we nearly had a fight develop between Sineido and Margarito. The former thought the latter had insulted his mother and started for the machete. When Don Alfredo intervened, this incident subsided in a deal of insults.

There was no water in the road after leaving the river. The poor arrieros who had sweated in the low grass of the river bottoms were nearly dead with thirst before they reached La Pita. One, Antonio, drank some water in a hole in the road, made by a mule's hoof, and as a result had diarrhoea. I gave him some bismuth, which he said helped.

As quickly as we got in, Rick climbed into his hammock and fell asleep, which with the quinine he has been taking, brought down his fever.

We all slept close together because of the trees. The usual tiger story pursues Rutherford. Don Alfredo told a harrowing one which happened near this very parage. A man was killed in a champa near here in a drunken brawl, and according to the law of the land they sent to Tenosique for the authorities to view the body before it was buried. It was ten days before they got back to examine the body, over which Don Alfredo had had a man and woman standing guard. The body lay in a ravine, and when the examination was over, they left it there. Shortly after they heard a noise and ran back to see what it was. They were just in time to see the corpus delicta being carried off by a large jaguar. They gave chase. The jaguar carried it up one hill and down the other side before he finally dropped it. When the cadaver was recovered, they found one leg had been gnawed off. With this and similar tales, the evening was passed until poor Rutherford was ready to believe anything.

May 6, Friday

A day from bad to worse. We got up at daylight and by 7:15 Don Alfredo, the five laborers, and I set out ahead to open the road. The rest of the party were to come on with the mulada.

Don Alfredo said we had to go back on the Libertad camino real for three-fourths of a league before we reached the turn off to Tres Marias. His

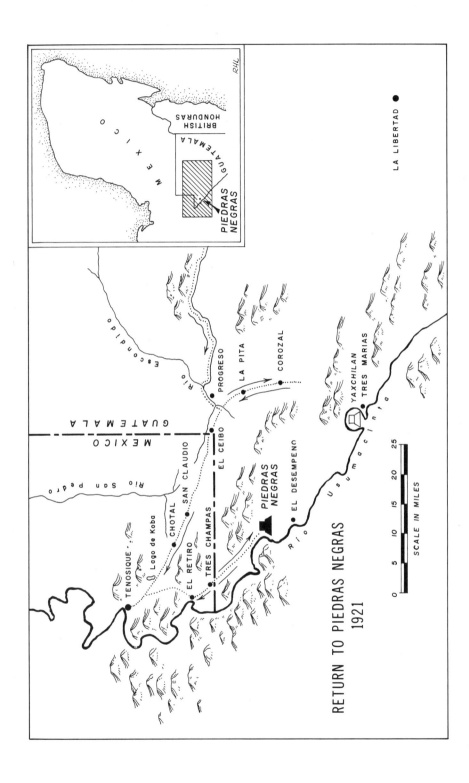

RETURN TO PIEDRAS NEGRAS
1921

SCALE IN MILES
0 5 10 15 20 25

MEXICO
GUATEMALA
BRITISH HONDURAS

PIEDRAS NEGRAS

TENOSIQUE
Lago de Koba
CHOTAL
EL RETIRO
TRES CHAMPAS
SAN CLAUDIO
EL CEIBO
PROGRESO
LA PITA
COROZAL
PIEDRAS NEGRAS
EL DESEMPEÑO
YAXCHILAN
TRES MARIAS
LA LIBERTAD

Rio San Pedro
Rio Escondido
Rio Usumacinta

RHL

estimates, I now know, are very low. It took us just two hours and five minutes to reach this point! We closed this road off well and then went on.

The road continued to the south. It was over very gently rolling country and was therefore fairly open. However, the boys had to cut around more than one fallen tree. We reached Corozal at 10:55, one hour and twenty-five minutes after leaving the Tenosique-La Libertad road.

We stopped here while the boys made *atole*. I wrote a note to the rear party that we were going on to Yaxchilan and to carry on. Just as we were leaving, the boys declared they heard the arrieros' cries and the blowing of a horn already coming up behind us. It was 12:00 when Muddy caught up, and the mulada was not far behind him. About this time also we began to encounter hills, the road gradually ascending. Soon we crossed an arroyo which had water in it, and from here our trouble began.

We were undoubtedly on the right road, but the country through which it passed was the most forsaken I have ever seen. It appeared to be a considerable range of limestone hills which I take to be the divide between the San Pedro and Usumacinta rivers, because the general trend of the range appeared to be running north and southeast. There was no difficulty in tracing the road over the hills, but between them were *akalches,* or stretches of low bush. I had never seen such thickets of vines, bejucos, creepers, and lianas. Where the road entered these, it was immediately lost. The only thing we could do was to cut through and look for the road on the other side. Time after time the boys did this, and always it was Joaquín who found the road. This slow, laborious, time consuming business went on practically all afternoon.

When we were in the depths of these akalches, occasionally the foliage was low enough to see through. Fairly high above us we could see hills. Before the afternoon was out we learned to long for them, since on them the road went fair and clear.

Over these divides and down into akalches, and over the down again, and so on all afternoon. Don Alfredo seemed to have no idea of the distance yet remaining to be covered. Still we wandered on always bearing south, the boys cutting through the terrible akalches.

Finally we gave up trying to reach Yaxchilan today and based our hopes on a water hole two leagues this side, which Don Alfredo said might have water. We passed this a little after 5:00. It was dry.

It then became apparent that we would have to make a dry camp. We tried to find a ramon tree, but without success. We finally picked out a place where there were some palms, and cleared a place of bush so that when the pack animals came in, there would be room to put the baggage.

We had just cleared this space when the mules began to struggle in. There was much confusion in the clearing when twenty-six mules were tied up.

May 7, Saturday

A day in which things went from worse to worst. Here we are sleeping at a water course some six leagues south of La Pita, have given up the idea of getting through by way of Tres Marias, and are on our way back to the Libertad–Tenosique road, which we will follow through to the vicinity of Tenosique and then out over to the Desempeño road. But everything in its place.

We got another splendid start. Everybody was thirsty and nobody was hungry, so we eliminated breakfast. I had given each group a tin of fruit last night to help quench their several thirsts. Don Alfredo, the five laborers, and I got off at 6:15. It was lucky we did so, for the road continued just as before. In fact, it steadily grew worse. That is the akalches were harder to get through and the little valleys up which we went were covered with denser bush. We soon began to lose our way.

Immediately after leaving the place where we slept, we passed an old parage which Don Alfredo remembered. After that it was quite obvious to me that he was confused as to just where the road did go. Time and time again he said it went one place, and Joaquín found it in another place. That we were on the road I could not doubt because of various signs in these passes through the hills. For instance, Chico called my attention to an old pack saddle abandoned by the road. Someone else noted an empty bottle, and Muddy pointed out the bones of a mule.

Three hours after we had left the camping place, Rutherford rode up and reported he had made it in just forty-five minutes. I calculated on this basis that we had done from three to three and a half miles. This distance had taken us one hundred and eighty minutes.

Just as Ricketson caught up, we reached a narrow canyon, and here we lost the road altogether. Twice Joaquín, Don Alfredo, and the other three boys tried to find it, but no luck. They got distinct traces up to a certain point and then lost them, nor could searching bring them to light.

Don Alfredo was obviously confused and knew not which way to turn, or indeed how far it was on ahead to the arroyo of Yaxchilan. He said from the point where we were lost, he calculated it was still two leagues to the Tres Marias-Desempeño road, or fifteen miles of such going. It was quite clear to me that neither mules nor men could stand it that long without water. The laborers had been drinking bejuca water all morning, and Chico had given me half a cup. It wasn't bad, but it was only a drop in a very big bucket to all the water we wanted and needed. A quick decision of some sort was necessary and a shift of plan imperative.

Don Alfredo offered to go on to open the road through, while we went back to the next water to camp until they came to advise us. But, with the road so overgrown, I doubt whether they could get through to the Tenosique-Desempeño-Tres Marias road in two days, and certainly not in one. Much as I hated to turn back it seemed to me that the longest way around was the shortest way home. I gave the word to him to get back as far as the first water and then camp for the night.

My plan is to hit the Tenosique-La Libertad road and go through to Tenosique, or near there, and then on the Desempeño road as far as Piedras Negras. This road is always traveled.

We turned back and gradually passed all the cargo animals except four, which, without arrieros, ran into the camping place ahead of me. The others came soon into the clearing. Oh, what a sorry mulada. Every pack required readjustment, and some of the animals lay down as if completely exhausted. It had taken me an hour and a quarter to cover coming back what had taken at least three and three quarters to do going out. At the most, we had made only four miles.

We left camp at 12:00 and were back where I am writing these lines at 1:50, but even though traveling hard we could not have covered more than nine miles all told.

We cleared a space for the cargoes as the animals began to straggle in. All were at camp by 3:00, and then we had tea. Never has liquid tasted better.

It is decided that we will sleep tomorrow night at Ceibo, about a kilometer from the Mexican boundary and the last parage in Guatemala on the Libertad-Tenosique road. Alfredo, with one man, will go into Progreso to get four quintals of corn and meet us tomorrow night at Ceibo, if he can make it. If not, he will go as far as he can and overtake us the next day. These are the plans, but who knows whether they will carry through. This country is so full of the unexpected. Moreover, as I write, the animals, which are not tied, keep coming back to water and then wander away from the ramonal. God knows how many we will have left in the morning when we get ready to start.

And now for a few notes on the geography of this benighted section of Petén. One thing I have noted in my five visits to the Department is this: chewing gum and archaeology always go hand in hand. That is to say, wherever you find ruins in any extent, you find the chico sapote abundantly. And wherever you find plenty of the chico sapote, there you find plenty of ruins. I have not noticed a single ruin since leaving Progreso and only two or three chico sapote trees. Nor do I think there are any considerable sites in these non-chicle bearing hills. On the map this western part of Petén, that region just east of the Usumacinta River, shows as a blank, unpopulated region. Now I know why.

It appears that there is a range of hills running roughly parallel with the Usumacinta on its eastern bank. This, I believe, is what forces the San Pedro River to make such a northerly bend before it comes into the Usumacinta River at Balancan.

This range, or series of ranges, must start somewhere between Balancan and Tenosique, running generally from northwest to southeast. We cut diagonally through the range on the unpleasant journey toward Tres Marias. The range is composed of limestone hills, with rather sharply rounded tops not more than two hundred feet from the general ground level; in places they are quite steep and are covered with trees. Between these are stretches of thick viney tangles, which give place to a higher vegetation as soon as the ascents are reached.

It will take a geologist to work out these several drainages in Petén, but I think I have a rough grasp on the general features. The Belize and its tributaries drain the eastern part of the Department. The Pasion rises in the Colony but flows south, southwest, west, and north again into the Usumacinta. The Usumacinta's eastern tributaries rise in the range of which I have just been speaking and run only short distances before reaching the Usumacinta; the San Pedro Martyr and the San Pedro Candelaria drain the northwestern corner and flowing generally westward into Mexico, the former into the Usumacinta below Balancan, the latter into the Bahia de Terminos.

Thus two rivers drain the whole northwest. The northeast is divided by tributaries of the Hondo River, Blue Creek, Booth River and the Bravo. I believe Ixcanrio is Booth River farther down, and the high divide known as the Sierra de Chunvis divides this system from the Belize system.

This leaves the interior lacustrine drainage: Yaxha and the lakes west of it, Petén Itzá itself, and the lakes north and west and the savannas which I believe must also have been old lake beds originally.

May 8, Sunday

A most unpleasant day, ending in a serious division and disruption of our mulada. The day started badly. When the mules were brought in, we only had fourteen, one over half.

At break of day Joaquín had heard a number of mules cross the arroyo and set off for Progreso. We all shouted warnings to the arrieros, but they insisted that the animals would not go far, and calmly let them go. Before 7:00 another nine mules had been found wandering in the bush south of the arroyo. A final count revealed four still missing, which all felt were well on their way back toward Progreso. Two animals and arrieros were sent on ahead to look for these four animals, while the rest of us sat down to wait. We waited and waited, cursing the negligence of the arrieros which permitted the mules to escape under their very noses.

About 9:45 Sineido and Antonio returned, reporting that they had seen the four mules just ahead of them a number of times, but when they tried to head them, the beasts galloped off. They chased the mules almost as far as La Pita, but were unable to grab them, so they returned.

I was determined to get started. We were six animals out, the four lost and the two which Alfred and Martin took to get the corn at Progreso. The caigo, including two pack saddles and three saddles, took up fourteen cargo animals. This left seven animals for riding, four for the arrieros and three for ourselves. With nothing for poor Muddy, Chico, and Don Alfredo, these three had to walk.

Rick and I left last. The last cargo animal fell down in crossing the arroyo and most unfortunate of all, it was No. 5, the photographic kyack, which got wet. This was completely submerged for a moment. There was no hope of examining it then, but we devoutly hoped it might have escaped a thorough drenching within. Rutherford thinks there were clothes packed on top, and if so, they may have absorbed what water leaked in.

We left at 11:23 and, to my disgust, had a number of akalches to ride through before we reached Corozal. I think it must be a fair two leagues, though it took us thirteen minutes under two hours to do it.

At 2:00 we passed the entrance for La Libertad, and at 4:00 we were back at La Pita, which we left day before yesterday. It was now only 4:00. As Don Alfredo had said it was just two leagues further to Ceibo, and thinking that Joaquín and his gang might be there ahead of us with a tree all felled, I had no hesitancy in saying, "Forward." I sent Miguel on to Progreso to advise Alfred that we were going on to Ceibo and to come in as soon as he could.

After leaving La Pita, our troubles started. Don Alfredo went ahead to stop the mules from turning down the Progreso road, and the mulada got off at 4:05 with Ricketson and me riding behind to see that nothing was lost. About a half league out, we came to the turn off. After some difficulty we persuaded the tail of our mulada to head in on the Ceibo trail. Immediately after getting in on it, the one-eared mule apparently began to peter out. Antonio announced it wouldn't last through to Ceibo. Rick gave up his riding animal for this cargo, and his saddle was changed to it. Rick took my animal, and I started to walk, but One-Ear actually trotted on ahead. I decided to catch him and ride, and he carried me through.

We rode and rode and rode. Don Alfredo had said it was only two leagues. Five, six, and seven, and still we continued. Meanwhile the heavy bush had given way to the low bush which borders the San Pedro River. I felt sure, when we reached this low bush, that we must be near the parage. But we were not.

Dusk began to fall, and still we wound around through this wretched low bush. I had Chico light the lantern, but it cast such a light all around that it made the going worse. Finally when he fell and put it out, I told him not to light it again. By this time we were reduced to two cargo animals and four saddle animals. We all kept close together, and we moved forward as fast as we might. About 7:15 we stumbled over some saddles and knew that another cargo animal had pitched its load and either gone on or hidden out in the bush.

We called ahead several times but got no answer. Finally we heard a faint shout and made sure that the mulada—what was left of it—had arrived at Ceibo. Our consternation may well be imagined when we found that we had reached nowhere, in fact that it was another dry camp. Indeed it was no camp at all, not even a clearing in the bush but only a place where Joaquín and his men had stopped when dusk began to fall!

Everybody was tired, cross, and hungry, and above everything else thirsty. However, there was no water. And a worse calamity was soon to develop.

A count of the cargo animals revealed that one had not come in. A frantic search ensued, in which it developed that it was the animal which had No. 5 kyack with the photographic outfit and the bundle with my cot, the table, and chairs. I was well disgusted, but there was no remedy. This makes the third time this season that I have been caught in this plight. I had Joaquín cut out the bush from behind where the kyacks had been unloaded and laid out my four kyacks here. Supper consisted of cheese, crackers, sardines and some tinned pineapple, a most indigestible compound.

Our situation is far from pleasant. One cargo, and that a very important one since it has the photographic outfit, is actually missing. Two are behind on the road, and all the men are dissatisfied. I think the blame may be placed equally on the shoulders of the arrieros who permitted the mules to escape last night in the direct face of my warning that they should tie the animals and upon Alfredo's shoulders for saying at 4:00 in the afternoon when we were at water at La Pita that it was only two leagues on to Ceibo, when it is at least four, if not five, leagues. This unfortunate calculation, or downright ignorance, on his part has caused the present fiasco.

Just before falling asleep, Don Alfredo said that we were sleeping at the same site where Geronimo Villanueva was killed. His brother had a montería at Tres Marias eight years ago when Joe and I were down the Usumacinta River. He is now Shufeldt's agent at Tenosique. As Manuel told it to me then, the arriero with whom Geronimo was traveling killed him, and some time later the mule of Don Geronimo came out at La Libertad. The mule which Don Alfredo now is riding is the same one. Out of all the bush, we strike upon this gloomy piece of the monte, replete with such dark memories, as our own stopping place.

May 9, Monday

Troubles continue. We lose more baggage.

Antonio and Sineido took two cargo animals back and brought in the pack of tinned goods and the saddles which had fallen by the wayside last night. In the meantime Don Alfredo had gone on to close off a right hand trail which leads to Progreso, but he returned to superintend the loading of the mules. It was decided that all possible cargo should be taken on ahead. We would send back for what had to be left. This amounted to the jack, the box of crackers, and four boxes of tinned goods, the corn grinder, and the saddles. The rest was loaded on twelve cargo animals, which we had three arrieros to operate.

Don Alfredo, Ricketson, and I went to the turn off to Progreso. Alfred left us to head off any mules wishing to turn in there, and Rick and I contin- ued to Ceibo. We had left the region of low bush and were now winding in and out among the spurs of the range which forces the San Pedro River northward. We had been going for some time when we came upon a cargo fallen by the road. They were Nos. 6 and 9, the former being Ricketson's, which caused him some dismay. Shortly after, we came to the mule which had done this thing, just about to dart off into the bush. Sineido stopped to tie it to a nearby tree, until some one could come back for it.

We continued for about another mile, and were almost at the conclusion that Don Alfredo had made another mistake, when we came to a bend in the road and on the right side through the bush saw the San Pedro River. Never was sight of water so welcome.

The Ceibo at which we had arrived was Ceibo, Petén, i.e. Guatemala. At first Don Alfredo contended that we were in Mexico, but we convinced him by compass, pencil, and location of the international monuments that we were still east of the line.

This place had been used as a montería by Don Eduardo Aguilera of Tenosique last year. There were a number of good champas. The boys had already appropriated one for us fronting on the river, which was a delightful location. It was very hot and an inferno of mosquitoes. As soon as the arrieros had had lunch, they went out again. Antonio and Margarito took their hammocks, pabellones, and food and set out to look for the mule lost last night. They were to go first to La Pita and then work back along the Pro- greso road.

Another great loss developed when all the cargoes were counted. We had started out with twelve cargoes this morning, but only eleven came in to Ceibo. It was quickly discovered that kyacks Nos. 2 and 12 are now missing. The former has all my books, drafting material, maps, and tobacco, and the latter has tinned foods. If these are lost, this will be a real calamity, besides which all that has gone before will have been as nothing.

Immediately after lunch Sineido set out to look for this animal which was lost between here and the branch where the Progreso road comes in. After 2:00 we heard shouts in the distance, and Alfred arrived with Martin, Miguel, six mules, and one hundred kilos of corn. They had seen no trace of either missing animal except that Alfredo had seen a fresh mule track in the savanna just beyond Ormigero, which had continued right up to where the La Pita road enters. After Miguel and Martin had eaten, I started them off again for the two cargoes left where we slept. About 9:15 in the evening they got lost in the bajo near here and left the cargo until morning. No signs of Antonio and Margarito. Do hope they will find the missing baggage. We are planted here until it is recovered.

May 10, Tuesday

A wasted day though no additional misfortunes and some good luck. I sent Sineido out this morning to look again for the lost mule and asked Miguel and Martin to bring in the two cargoes from the bajo where they had left them last night. I settled down to writing in my diary. Just before noon Alfred said, "Here comes the motor," and in another ten minutes a boat had pulled up to the shore. I decided to get a guide from it who knew the Tenosique road and also to send a note on to Shufeldt.

There were two men aboard, an old chap named Tacho Mai and a younger man named Genaro. The former, having been the mail man, is the best informed man as to roads south and west of Tenosique, but unfortunately he is carrying a special message from Manuel Villanueva to Shufeldt and could not come. The younger man would come, however. I had him in the champa and quickly made satisfactory financial arrangements with him.

I wrote next to Shufeldt telling him of our several misfortunes and while I was thus employed, Margarito and Antonio came with the lost cargo, the photograph kyack and the bundle of cot, chairs, and tables. I was very thankful for this. At least we can go ahead with our photographic program, and the furniture will not come amiss.

By this time I had finished my letter and bidding us goodby, Don Pepe put out and soon disappeared around a bend of the river, towing the familiar trio—the Maria, the Pluma, and the Aurora—behind.

Sineido returned and reported no luck in finding the mule. I was indignant, and after lunch I started him and Antonio with grub and instructions to go through to Progreso if necessary in order to bring back the cargo and the animals.

After 4:00, when the mosquitoes and heat were at their height, we all went in bathing; much fun ensued at Ruddy's expense in his efforts to learn swimming. He insisted upon having a huge rope tied around his waist with the other end anchored to a tree on the bank. He would then spring in, and when he felt he was going under, he would gargle, pull, and I would drag him back to shore. This bath has been a delightful feature of the enforced stop at Ceibo. It is one of the few things I will look back upon with pleasure.

May 11, Wednesday

Our good luck continues. The new man, Genaro, proved his worth by going out early this morning and finding the two missing kyacks. This was great news, as it means the map on which I worked so hard and long is not lost.

May 12, Thursday

The plan of the day was that Ricketson and I go ahead with Genaro, Joaquín, and his four men to find the trail, close off side roads, and open around fallen trees. We got off at 7:15 and in fifteen minutes were back on the main La Libertad-Tenosique road. We turned to the right and at 7:50 crossed into Mexico. The boundary is marked by a tall concrete obelisk with two bronze tablets, one saying MEXICO on the western side and the other GUATEMALA on the eastern side. Ten minutes later we passed some low bush and a number of lime trees, which were on the site of Ceibo, Mexico, now quite abandoned. I have entered Mexico at many places on its southern and eastern frontier, but I think this point the most out of the way place of all.

The country appeared to be a succession of low ridges over which we crossed; our general direction seemed to be northeast. Two hours out we passed three well defined mounds, two on the left and one on the right, the last a pyramid. Fifteen minutes later we found ourselves at an old chicleria with one long champa. There were several roads leading out from this with the result that before we finally found the Tenosique road, we had lost another half hour. I wrote a note and left it on a forked stick saying we were going on the three remaining leagues to San Claudio.

As we arrived at San Claudio, Genaro signalled to us to bring a gun. There was a large peccary about two hundred feet off drinking at the aguada. Unfortunately Ricketson had no cartridges for his gun, so he used his .45 army automatic. The first shell only went off at the cap. When the second was fired, it jammed. With the sound of this, the peccary gave a great jump and made off through the bush to be seen no more.

The parage was far from attractive. There were no champas, and some rank stiff bushes grew all over the clearing. The day had been almost insupportable with intense heat. The perspiration just dropped off me. And the mosquitoes were hell. We were thus well heated when we got to the parage and then we fell to making a clearing, which finished us off. Both canteens were empty, and our thirst was very great. But there was nothing to do but wait for the rest of the party to arrive.

Meanwhile it had been thundering a great deal and clouds were piling up overhead. It looked like rain, and the excessive heat and high humidity made it almost certain. It had not rained for so long that most felt it would not do so now. Ricketson and I were the only ones to sleep under the tarp, and the only ones to remain dry when the heavy rainstorm broke at a little before 11:00. I wonder if this is the first of the rainy season. If so, we will be out of luck at Piedras Negras.

May 13, Friday

Another change of plan made necessary by the events of the morning. When I told Joaquín to do something, he went off in a huff, firing himself and his four men, including the old rascal who is cooking for his gang. These men are all from Balancan. I understand from what Muddy and Don Alfred tell me they have overheard that they have never intended to go to Piedras Negras at all, but have intended to go to Tenosique from the nearest point to there we reached.

Their departure left me a double quandary. In the first place, it leaves me without men to work at the ruins. In the second place, it would have placed me in an awkward position with the Tenosique authorities. Had these fellows gone into Tenosique with the word that a mulada of twenty-seven animals and sixteen cargoes was passing through the corner of Mexico from Ceibo to Tres Champas without calling at Tenosique, we would probably have a mounted troop overtake us long before we reach Tres Champas and force us to return to Tenosique to explain ourselves. So certain I am of this that I have changed plans. We will go directly to Tenosique.

This will quiet any yarn these men may have circulated that we are evading the authorities and enable me to find out from Don Manuel Villanueva how conditions are there. If we can get out of Tenosique on Monday the 16th, we will be in Piedras Negras not later than Wednesday, the 18th. We can have ten to twelve days there and get back to Tenosique on the 31st of May or the 1st of June.

We changed the order of march for today. Muddy, Ruddy, Chico, and Alfred went forward with the guide and one pack animal. The arrieros strung along behind, and the last two got off at 8:56. We pulled in behind them.

The road continued over the low hills and after about an hour out, crossed a long low muddy plain with high bush. At 12:00 we came to the abandoned ranch of Chotal, where there was a small arroyo with water in it. From this time on, water became more plentiful.

Also from Chotal we followed what must have been a good wide road once cleared through the bush. This is now badly grown up, but we could and did follow along it for considerable stretches at a time. It was almost straight, wide, and well cleared enough to have been a mahogany track pass.

About 3:30 the land broke away suddenly to the east. We saw the Lake of Koba, possibly two miles long, judging from what I saw of it through the trees. There was a destroyed champa at the southern end, but skirting around the western side, we reached our parage, just seven hours and ten minutes after starting.

May 14, Saturday

At 10:00 this morning we rode into Tenosique, a large rambling place covering quite an area but with a population of not more than thirty-five hundred. Some of the houses were of stone. A few had lamina roofs, but most were thatched with guano. After several turns, Genaro led us down a street which ran toward the river. We soon reached Manuel Villanueva's house, a somewhat pretentious building as the houses here go.

Word had been received from Balancan that the *Clara Ramos*, with General Mineda aboard, would get in about midnight, and the town was getting ready for his reception. That night the moving about of people caused the dogs to bark practically all the time. At midnight the crowd having assembled, they gave "vivas" for the general and added to the confusion. But it was not until 2:30 that a loud whistle announced the arrival of the *Clara Ramos*.

At the same moment a number of guns were shot off, a band burst into music, and the crowd cheered.

May 16, Monday

After taking a great deal of time, so as not to break the general rule that on the first day of a trip a late start must be made, we finally got off at 10:30. At first the going was over the river plain. We passed the cemetery which has a new brick front wall, with the back and sides fenced with barbed wire. About a kilometer out we passed the first arroyo, and at noon we crossed the Poliva, a small stream now but obviously a good sized arroyo in the rainy season. We stopped here ten minutes to fix the cargoes. Everything is coming along nicely.

We think that we have a good outfit this time. There is a notable difference in the manner of the men, who are more jolly and cheerful. The laborers, of whom we have six, actually helped the arrieros unload when we camped. Our mulada consists of twenty-one animals.

We left the Poliva at noon and soon began to ascend a series of low rises, which are the foothills of the range we passed through yesterday. Coming down into one of these steep little arroyos, I got a fall which might have proved serious if not fatal, but which happily only gave me a blow on the knee.

We were riding down into a little ravine when my saddle went over my mule's head and threw me into the ravine on my neck. I rolled aside as quickly as I could, in case the mule should follow, but he held his own above. I picked myself up and limped around. Estanislas was far ahead, but I called him back. He was most solicitous, even to the point of offering me his fast diminishing bottle of aguardiente to bathe my knee.

At 2:00 we reached a large clearing with several guano houses which comprised the ranch called Tepiscuintla. A woman was working about under an open shed. We waited here until the mulada came up to see if the head arriero wanted to continue any farther or not. When he arrived, he said we would stop for the night at the arroyo of Saya, a half a league farther on. We reached there in another forty minutes.

There were no champas but there was a clearing in the bush overgrown with an herb or grass which is used for flavoring soup in Yucatán [cilantro].

May 17, Tuesday

We left Saya at 8:30 and began soon to go over some steep limestone ridges, in fact, I think I can safely say we saw more limestone outcroppings today than in the previous four months combined.

El Retiro, a parage we later reached, is supposed to be half way from Tenosique to Piedras Negras. We left there at 1:20, and went up a long steep hill. This I can say without any exaggeration was the longest and steepest we have encountered in the entire trip. It was almost straight up in places over outcroppings of the native limestone. At Estanislas's suggestion, we waited behind the mulada here to urge it up the hill. When we reached the top at last, Estanislas and one of the arrieros stayed behind to close up a narrow place between two steep rocks so that in case the mules escape from the parage, they can not get beyond this point on the road back to Tenosique.

In the middle of the afternoon we camped at a parage which was notable for lack of insects.

May 18, Wednesday

At 8:30 this morning we came to a clearing on our trail called El Pabellon, through which we were told the Guatemalan border passed, and we were again back in Petén. For the next two hours we passed through a heavily forested but level plain. The mountains here must make a big bend away from the river. At least we struck no steep hills in this stretch, which was level and correspondingly easy going.

Finally at 12:30 we crossed over a range of hills and came down through the ruins to the big ceibo tree, which Maler marks on his map, and which was formerly the old parage of Piedras Negras. This enclosed for me a tremendous stretch of territory, all of western Petén in fact, since Joe Spinden and I had come into Piedras Negras from the south in 1914. Now here I was approaching it from the north.

We did not tarry here but cut our way through to the river. We tied our horses on a sand bank and looked around for a camp site, selecting one on a bench in the hill well above the usual high water mark of the Usumacinta and under the shade of some heavy trees. In the meantime the laborers had arrived. We put them to felling all the underbrush, and soon had a large clearing. Muddy gave us a lunch and afterward leaving the others to finish getting the clearing made for camp, I took Estanislas and Martin with me to look for the ruins.

We followed the arroyo back to the ceibo tree and then back along the Tenosique trail until we were about opposite the ruins. Here Estanislas picked up an old picado, and following this in, we came presently to a large stela which I identified as No. 14.

With this as a starter, it did not take us long to locate the other monuments at this group, Stelae 12, 13, 16, 17, 18 and 19. I did not locate Stela 15, nor did Joe and I seven years ago. We did no clearing here, my only idea in coming out at all being to locate as many monuments as possible today so we could get to work tomorrow without loss of time. I thought I would let the far group go (Stelae 1-11) until tomorrow, and find the others (Stelae 22-27) between where we were and the river.

We started out from the middle group to do this. Presently Estanislas picked up an old picado which we followed. This bent so much to the right, however, that I knew it was leading us to the far group after all. Sure enough, we began to ascend a hill soon, skirting an arroyo on our left and finally climbed up over a steep terrace to find ourselves in front of the stairway between Stelae 9-11 on the left and Stelae 1-8 on the right.

We returned to Stelae 12-19 and set out again to look for Nos. 22-37 which we had missed. But we turned too far to the right and came into a ravine which eventually brought us out to the river below camp. We climbed along the rocky shore so that when I got back to camp, I was all in.

The mulada was in, and Muddy had a fine camp already fixed. After a good supper, I made preparations to retire almost at once, being not only very tired but also well aware of the strenuous day we are going to have ahead of us tomorrow. Everybody quickly followed.

May 19, Thursday

This was the first day of work at the ruins, what Estanislas, Martin, and I accomplished yesterday afternoon being little more than a location of the monuments so that we could find where we were. The plan of operations was this: Chico was to stay in camp and help Rutherford build a photographic champa down by the river. Muddy was to make our own camp more livable. Yesterday we had done hardly more than fell the underbrush and put up the tarp. All the rest of us were to open up paths between the different groups of monuments, as well as the monuments within the groups, so that they will be more easily reached.

Instead of cutting through the bush direct to the city from camp, we went back up the arroyo to the Tenosique-Desempeño road and then back along that until we were behind some of the mounds of the city. Here we left the road and struck into the bush to the left.

Once over this line of mounds, instead of turning to the right which would have brought us to Stelae 12-19 which we found yesterday, I had the boys turn to the left to see if we could encounter Stelae 22-37. They scattered through the bush in this general direction, and soon a shout advised that something had been found. It was Stelae 25 and 26, and soon 24, 27, and 28 were located. Quickly afterwards they found 29, 30, and 31.

Meanwhile Alfred had gone around this court from Stela 31, and picked up Stela 32, Stela 33, and Stela 34. I went over there and found the other three, Nos. 35-37.

While I was cleaning around these monuments, Ricketson had been looking for the shortest way to camp. He returned presently, saying that it would not be more than ten minutes to camp. I gave him Martin, and the two of them opened up a trail between the mound of Stela 28 and that of Stelae 29-31. When we walked through this going back to lunch, it only took us five minutes. While he and Martin were cutting this road through to camp, I had the boys gather the large bottom fragments of Stela 29 and assemble them with the top fragments which Maler in 1899 had brought down to the platform in front. By the time this work was done, it was only 11:00. I sent Estanislas and Martin to find the middle group of monuments (Stelae 12-19).

We waited at the northwest corner of the Southern Plaza (plaza of Stelae 24-37) until they shouted that they had found the other group. Then from both ends we started opening up a trail. As this was to be a main thoroughfare of communication while we are here, I had it particularly well made, wide and fairly cleared.

While the cuadrilla under Estanislas was cleaning around these monuments, Ricketson and I set out to look for Stelae 20, 21, 22, and 23. We picked up the first two quickly enough, though I very much doubt whether either of them was ever a stela. Ricketson next found Stela 22 where it should be, and soon after, Stela 23. I was not sure at first that Stela 23 was Maler's 23, but I came to the conclusion that it could be no other. It was now noon, and we returned to camp satisfied with the first half day's work.

Rutherford said that he and Chico had built a champa by the water's edge where he was getting fixed for the photographic work. Muddy, on his part, had got camp looking more homelike and convenient. If it doesn't rain too hard, we will do very well here.

After lunch Ricketson and I again took our cuadrilla back to the group of Stelae 12-19 and started making a new road to the far group, Maler's Acropolis. This is really not far off. When we came home tonight, it took me just fifteen minutes from the stairway between Stelae 1-8 and Stelae 9-11 to camp. I should estimate it by trail as not more than three quarters of a mile.

We connected these two groups with a well defined trail and spent the rest of the afternoon bathing and cleaning the several fragments into which Stela 1 and Stela 8 have broken. I had all the boys at work on these pieces, with the result that before we quit, I had a good idea as to the general condition of these eight stelae and the large round altar (No. 1) in front of them.

This was hot work. When we got back to camp, four of us went in bathing in the river. The water was wonderfully refreshing. We all agreed that this daily bath will be one of the most delightful features of our life here.

May 20, Friday

A big red letter day full of remarkable discoveries. It was only the first day of intensive work, since yesterday was a preliminary day of cleaning and locating the monuments.

The work was divided into three parts. Ricketson and Alfred, with two *mozos,* devoted themselves to clearing lines of sight, prior to starting the measuring. Rutherford, four of the men, and Chico worked on assembling the monuments. Rutherford decided to get these all together first and then do the photographing at one fell blow. I had one mozo, Martin. My work consisted in drawing all the inscriptions I could in the time available. All three parties started at the south group, or that nearest the camp.

I drew the Initial and Supplementary Series on Stela 37 which took the greater part of the morning. The date I had already deciphered seven years ago as 9.12.0.0.0 [A.D. 672]. Before dinner I also drew the two glyphs on the round column (Altar No. 6) between Stelae 34 and 35. Yesterday when I found this, I thought it was a new discovery, but on reading Maler last night, I observed that he had located this altar, though he had failed to note the two glyphs on it. All that is left of these are their two coefficients, both expressed as very large head variants. The first is clearly 5 and the second 3. It cannot be mere coincidence therefore that the terminal date of the next hotun ending to Stela 35 is 5 *Ahau* 3 *Zac*, i.e. 9.11.5.0.0. 5 *Ahau* 3 *Zac* [A.D. 657]. In fact, I think there can be no doubt but that this is the date of this altar or column. This was the last thing I did before lunch.

In the meantime Rutherford had been assembling the broken fragments of Stela 35 and later 37. After lunch, he returned to the stelae of the west group and put in the rest of the afternoon there.

I drew the Initial Series and Supplementary Series on Stela 35, which took me well on toward the close of the afternoon, and was thus employed when Ricketson and Alfred came up with the news of a wonderful discovery. Alfred, in scouting around at the far group, had found two new stelae, each having inscriptions on their sides. Although I was busy enough, I had to go to see them.

At first I believed these might be 9.15.15.0.0 [A.D. 746] still missing, and a stela for 9.16.0.0.0 [A.D. 751] only represented by Altar 2. But I decided since there were two, the most likely hotuns would be 9.12.5.0.0 [A.D. 677] and 9.12.10.0.0 [A.D. 682], both still not accounted for.

On our way there we passed Stela 26. The light was falling across its side so that it brought out the fact that it had an Initial Series on the left side, and though most of the coefficients were missing, happily the terminal date was very clear as 8 *Ahau* 13 *Cumhu*. By turning to my notebook, I found this date was none other than 9.9.15.0.0 8 *Ahau* 13 *Cumhu* [A.D. 628], just one katun later than the stela next to it. This is a fine new early date and fits in with the sequence of hotun markers we are building up here.

From here, we passed the middle group where Rutherford and his men were at work. They are doing splendid work, and had Stela 14 fitted together. From Stela 16 they had cut a due west line through to the far group. Before reaching this, however, we turned off to the right, i.e., north, and after circling this last high plaza, we came to two tremendous monuments. Both had fallen face upward.

The first had its Initial Series on the left side facing it, and the coefficients were in bars and dots. The date was beautifully clear as 9.12.5.0.0 3 *Ahau* 3 *Xul* [A.D. 677]. This was one of my first pair of dates. We went at once to the other, which I knew must be 9.12.10.0.0 9 *Ahau* 18 *Zotz* [A.D. 682]. This was somewhat more difficult to decipher as it was like Stela 37 in having large head variant glyphs. The 12 head and the 10 head were fairly clear and the 9 of the 9 *Ahau* also showed. There could be no doubt as to either date. We named them Stela 38 and Stela 39.

We were tired and returned to camp after these discoveries. Rutherford came in with his gang shortly afterward. Ricketson and I were the only two who went down to the river for a bath. We noticed that the water level had dropped a lot in the past two days.

After supper Ricketson and Alfred worked on their map and I on the calculations on Stela 35. The Initial Series I finally worked out as 9.11.9.8.6 12 *Cimi* 9 *Cumhu*. The big discovery of the day, of course, is that of the two new monuments, Stelae 39 and 38. This means that after completing Stela 37 in the south plaza in 9.12.0.0.0, the people of Piedras Negras moved up to the far group. At the next hotun ending, there they put up Stela 39. From then on for seventy five years there is only one hotun marker now missing: 9.15.15.0.0 [A.D. 746]. It now makes a very remarkable sequence, in fact the most remarkable and complete sequence yet found anywhere.

It looked something like rain, but it did not come down. How much longer will it hold off?

May 21, Saturday

A rather slow-moving day. I started work on Stelae 33 and 34, but as soon as the light was sufficient, I drew Stela 31. The inscription on the top of this is in shocking condition. Rarely have I seen a text more effaced by weathering without actually being gone. I had to make the identification on the basis of the month glyph, which is fortunately quite clear as 3 *Pax*. If this is a hotun ending, it occurs at 9.10.5.0.0 7 *Ahau* 3 *Pax* [A.D. 638] and cannot recur for 949 tuns. Since at this position it fits so well with the other stelae in this same court, I think there cannot be any doubt that this is its date.

Rutherford had finished turning all the stelae we are going to photograph in this court, and he was ready for more work. So I accompanied him to Stelae 22 and 23. There was nothing to do on Stela 22, but on Stela 23 it was a delicate piece of assemblage. To begin with, it was by no means certain that all the fragments were parts of one and the same stela. In falling this monument had broken first into three large fragments. The top then broke into two pieces, one large and one small. The middle section was broken into ten or fifteen pieces but lay as it fell. It looked to me as though it had been cracked by a tree growing on top of it. With considerable difficulty the boys assembled this monument. It has two Initial Series, a very unusual feature occurring on less than ten other monuments everywhere. I could not decipher this today, but I believe it probably records the date 9.16.10.0.0 1 *Ahau* 3 *Zip* [A.D. 761].

After lunch I took Rutherford and his men up to the far group to the two new stelae, 38 and 39. He is to assemble these first.

On returning to Stela 25 where Martin was waiting, Alfred and Ricketson soon came with the news that they had found a new stela, number 42. This evidently stood just next to Stela 29, the bottom of which I had moved yesterday. It had a round top and had broken into three pieces with every·

appearance of having fallen face down. As the sides were plain, we had great hopes of finding a carving in good condition on the bottom side. Ricketson, Alfred, Martin and I turned the top fragment, and our chagrin was large when we discovered that it was quite plain. It seems likely now that the face that had fallen up was the sculptured front.

I returned to Stelae 25 and 26. I drew the Initial Series of the latter, which as I recorded yesterday is 9.9.15.0.0 8 *Ahau* 13 *Cumhu.* Although the light was getting poor, I turned next to the Initial Series of Stela 25 and finished it before I had to give up on account of the failing light.

Rutherford's work is developing a crop of blows. Ramiro Pino Suarez, who is the nephew of the Pino Suarez who was Vice President of Mexico during Francisco Madero's presidency, sustained a painful blow on the foot from a stone while he was working yesterday. This morning before lunch while at work on Stela 23 Luciano got a bad pinch from a stone. Ricketson dressed Ramiro's toe this morning and Luciano's finger this noon. The latter's nail has already turned black, and he will surely lose it.

May 22, Sunday

Today was anything but a day of rest. Everybody worked at top speed, and Ricketson made a splendid discovery.

I began the day with Stela 25, which I had not quite finished yesterday afternoon. After this was done, I took all the necessary measurements on Stelae 24, 26, and 27. Martin, who is turning into a good assistant, and I next moved over to Stelae 22 and 23. The former never seems to have had an Initial Series, though a period ending date of 8 *Ahua* 8 *Zotz.* The end of a hotun surely fixes its position in Maya chronology as 9.16.5.0.0 [A.D. 756]. It did not take us long to draw this, and we then moved over to the large fine stela, No. 23. In spite of the fact that this has two Initial Series, one on each side, I could not date it. Both are in a shocking condition. The limestone is soft and rubs off with a brush. There are some Secondary Series left in the panel of sixty-four glyphs at the bottom of the front or back side, whichever it is, that I may be able to decipher. All I could do this morning was to make notes on them.

While I was drawing here, I heard halloos in the bush as two men with guns approached. They were living at Porvenir northwest of here on the river. This being Sunday, they were out on a hunting trip. They stayed for awhile watching my drawing and asked where the mines were located! Of course, they cannot even conceive of anyone so crazy as to waste his time over "old stones."

I was still here when Ricketson and Alfred came with the fine news that they had discovered one or two new stelae on beyond Stelae 9 and 10. As I had not found Stela 11 the first afternoon, I felt surely that one of these must be it, but Alfred thought both were new. One, however, I knew at once was the missing stela 9.15.15.0.0 [A.D. 746]. As Alfred was going back again up to this far group after lunch, I decided to wait until later to go see it. I finished Stela 23 before lunch and got a good start on Stela 12.

The only date that is now open for Stela 23 is 9.16.10.0.0 [A.D. 761] five years after the date of Stela 22, since Stela 16 at the last group records 9.16.15.0.0 [A.D. 766]. I think there is very little doubt but that this monument belongs to this period ending.

Immediately after lunch I went with Alfred to the far west group and saw his new monuments. One was Stela 11, as I had suspected. For one minute I feared his other might be a part of it as it lay on the slope of the terrace nearby and lower than the fragments of Stela 11 above. I started Martin cleaning the top, and he soon uncovered another larger fragment. Alfred and I measured the two, which were fifteen feet eight inches long. Our line probably is a little short, but it will easily reach sixteen feet. This monument, to which we gave the name Stela 40, had glyphs on its side. At once I called Ruddy and his gang and started them digging around its sides.

Chico and Martin dug down on the left side and uncovered the Initial Series. This starts out 9.15, the tuns are not clear, but the uinals are 9, and the day coefficient is 11. At the bottom of this side, the last glyph is 9 *Ahau*. This is the day of the terminal date, or 9.15.15.0.0 9 *Ahau* 18 *Xul* [A.D. 746]. I am satisfied later Secondary Series on either this side or the other side will bring it up to 9.15.15.0.0.

While Ruddy and his men were getting the jack placed, Alfred and I climbed the high hill behind Stelae 9, 10, 11, and 40, and turning to the right, worked over behind the stairway between this mound and the one behind Stelae 1-8. What a welter of buildings! There were several succeeding terraces, each higher than the other. We passed old Maler's Casa Grande, which Ricketson and Alfred make out to be one hundred fifty feet long.

Climbing still higher, we passed around the crest of the hill, and saw the river below us. This is the hill we saw from camp which makes the river turn to the left around it. We calculate its base is about a thousand feet from the Roca de Sacrificios.

Before returning to the work at Stela 40, I went to Alfred's two stelae, 38 and 39. Rutherford's men had made a good job assembling these, and both monuments showed up very clearly. The inscription of Stela 39 (9.12.5.0.0 or A.D. 677) is in the better condition, but there is no doubt about Stela 38 being 9.12.10.0.0 or A.D. 682. I found the day of the terminal date 9 *Ahau* repeated as the last glyph. Both unfortunately fell face up and are badly destroyed in consequence. Stela 39 has a figure in full front presentation, but the features of the face are partially destroyed.

After looking these monuments over, we returned to Stela 40. Ruddy and his men were making good headway in getting it ready to turn over, but as I had a lot of work to do on Stela 14, I did not tarry but returned to that monument. It grew so dark in the bush by 5:00 that I gave up trying to finish Stela 14 and came back to camp.

Being a feast day, our turkey from Desempeño had been sacrificed for the evening meal. It tasted good to get fresh meat again.

May 23, Monday

The work continues to go forward satisfactorily. These Tenosiqueros are by all odds the best bunch of laborers we have had anything to do with yet. Under Ruddy's supervision, they are assembling the monuments in fine shape.

I started out the day on Stela 14, finished my work there, and before noon also drew the Initial Series and Supplementary Series on Stelae 13 and 16.

Words fail me to describe adequately the beauties of the new monument, Stela 40. Ruddy had both pieces turned over on their backs and the sculptured face turned up. It was practically in mint state and the most delicate details of the carving perfectly preserved. The composition is a principal figure kneeling facing to the left. He kneels on top of a very large human head only drawn as far as the breast. The details are extraordinarily preserved. The delicate lining of the hair, the fabric-like treatment of the headdress, and small beads on the necklace are all as perfect as the day they were carved. Rutherford will, of course, photograph the front of this.

Of the group of stelae in front of Temple 5 (Stelae 32-37 inclusive) all are now dated save Stela 32, and I think there can be but little doubt but that this dates from 9.10.15.0.0 6 *Ahau* 13 *Mac* [A.D. 647]. This makes the Series as follows:

Stela 38	9.10.10.0.0	A.D. 642		Stela 35	9.11.10.0.0	A.D. 662
Stela 32	9.10.15.0.0	A.D. 647		Stela 36	9.11.15.0.0	A.D. 667
Stela 34	9.11.0.0.0	A.D. 652		Stela 37	9.12.0.0.0	A.D. 672
Altar 6	9.11.5.0.0	A.D. 657				

These, added to the discoveries of Stelae 38, 39, and 40, and the allotment of Stelae 14, 17, 18, and 19 to the hotuns from 9.17.5.0.0 [A.D. 775] to 9.18.0.0.0 [A.D. 790] inclusive, leaves not a single gap between 9.9.15.0.0 [A.D. 628] and 9.18.5.0.0. [A.D. 795] except for 9.10.0.0.0 [A.D. 633] which I think it is almost certain was recorded on the large, fine Stela 30.

May 25, Wednesday

Just five more days of work. I finished three more monuments today. At this rate I will just get through Sunday night. Rutherford started his photograph taking today and made fair progress.

Of all our activities, the map is the most forward. In fact, Ricketson says that it is practically done except for a few measurements. He and Alfred have done splendid work on it and have every cause to feel proud of the result. The Maler map is extraordinarily inaccurate. He shows no plazas at all, and Ricketson finds that the city groups into three well defined units: the western group including the Acropolis; Stelae 1 to 11 inclusive, Stelae 38 and 39 and Altars 1 and 2.

Just after Martin and I got back to the ruins after lunch, we heard a faint hallooing off on the Tenosique road. It was Don Manuel's mulada on its way to Desempeño with supplies for the mahogany workers who are going into the bush for a fifteen day journey up to the headwaters of the Salinas River. The poor devils are signed on for a year. We were chiefly interested in the mulada because it brought some supplies for us.

Two mounds at the northern group have excited my liveliest curiosity. They are parallel, face each other, and each has a platform in front of it. In shape and arrangement they so forcibly suggest a ball court that I am going to have them excavated tomorrow. If they are the sides of a ball court, we ought to find the rings. We have always held that *tlachtli* was an Axtec game, but it might have originated in the Maya area. It would be a spectacular study if we could turn up one or the other of these rings.

May 27, Friday

Work continues, but there is so much to be done that I have decided to stay another day. That is, we will leave here Tuesday, the 31st, instead of Monday, the 30th.

Showers in the afternoon slowed up work again. I do not mind the getting wet, but drawing simply couldn't be done under sprinkling conditions. In spite of these handicaps, however, I did my daily stint of three monuments, Stelae 1, 3, and 5. I did 5 the first thing in the morning. It is very simple—bar and dot numerals—and clearly declares the date 9.14.5.0.0 [A.D. 716]. Also did Stela 3 in the morning. This is equally clear as 9.14.0.0.0 [A.D. 711] but took considerably more time as so much of the detail is still preserved: cross hashure, double-lining, etc. After lunch I started on Stela 1, which has large numerals like Stelae 37 and 38 except that they are in bars and dots. This went fairly rapidly and the date is again clear as 9.13.15.0.0 [A.D. 707].

On the way back to camp I went by Stelae 32-37 and found Rutherford had been digging in a drain at the north end of the platform. To my delight and amazement, he had found a fragment of stone with glyphs, which had been used to cover the drain. The glyph side was not down but on one edge. I did not see anything decipherable as I passed tonight, but it was late. One thing very noticeable is that the glyphs are all incised, a feature I have noted nowhere else here save possibly on Stela 30. I could not determine whether this is part of a lintel or a stela. It is interesting as showing the secondary usage which was so prevalent at Copán.

May 28, Saturday

Because Ricketson had finished at the ball court (?), I decided to have him dig out the drain thoroughly, in hopes we might find some more fragments of the monument that Rutherford uncovered there yesterday. He went there with me. I gave it a closer examination, which was amply rewarded. I recognized first Glyph C of the Supplementary Series, then Glyph A, and then the month 18 *Tzec* very clearly. After this came the well known hand ending sign with all the regular elements present, and after it, half a glyph which was the end of katun 5. I thought I remembered that katun 5 ended on 18 *Tzec,* but I was so excited I sent one of the boys back to camp to bring Goodman's tables. When he returned, I looked it up and saw that the date was 9.5.0.0.0 11 *Ahau* 18 *Tzec* [A.D. 534]. This made this fragment the oldest dateable object in the city by seventy five years, the next oldest being Stela 25, 9.8.15.0.0 [A.D. 608].

At this point I had an inspiration. I remembered that the glyphs on Stela 30 are incised, and also that part of its inscription is missing. We hastily measured this fragment and went across the court to Stela 30 and measured it. Both were the same thickness, and this fragment was the right shape to fill the missing part of Stela 30. I had the boys carry it over to 30, and it fitted.

This was real luck. It gives me the date of that monument, which is the oldest yet recovered from the city. It makes the dated occupation of Piedras Negras extend for more than two and a half centuries, i.e. from 9.5.0.0.0 to 9.18.5.0.0 [A.D. 534-795].

The evening closed in lowering and threatening. It came on to rain early and increased in violence. The thunder rolled, the lightning played, and down came the rain heavier than ever. The bush to me is cheerless enough at best, but when it is dripping wet, it is all but impossible.

May 29, Sunday

I had thought to make this my last day of drawing. The weather conditions were excellent too, with only a little sprinkle all day long. But I had bitten off too much and did not complete my program.

I started on Stela 6 and soon finished it. In order to save time, I had lunch sent out for Martin and me. Rutherford had the same done for himself and Diego, who has been helping him. About 9:00 I had finished with Stela 6 and began on the four legs of Altar 2. Each one of these has nine glyph blocks, and I had drawn the calendric ones in 1914, though not to scale. Though time was pressing, I decided to draw the whole thing over again. Rutherford had had a great clearing made around it, and the light conditions were excellent.

The first thing I discovered when I gave it close examination was that it had had an Initial Series. This could be made out in spite of almost complete effacement due to the rains of fifteen centuries. I knew from my work of seven years ago that the date of this altar was 9.16.0.0.0 2 *Ahau* 13 *Tzec* [A.D. 751] and it did not surprise me therefore to find this date repeated as the Initial Series on the front of this altar.

This brings the number of Initial Series here at Piedras up to thirty four, the largest number, next to Copán, of any city in the Maya area.

The river has risen very considerably. The rocks from which we used to go in swimming are now completely submerged. The water too has changed color completely since we came. It was green at first, but it is now muddy. It is wonderfully refreshing nonetheless, and for the hundredth time today we blessed its proximity to camp—seventy-five yards run down hill in the sand and splash!

Of all the camps during the past four months I shall look back upon this as the most delightful. The cool refreshing river a stone's throw off, an open vista to lovely hills across in Mexico, and an absence of ticks and fleas. Thrice blessed spot!

May 31, Tuesday

Everyone was up early. It was 4:40 when I rose myself. The arrieros had been up a good hour then. It did not take me long to pack my single kyack, and we sat down to breakfast before 6:00.

The plans for the day were these: Estanislas Reyes was to stay behind with me, while the others were to go on ahead as soon as they could get off.

Estanislas and I set off for the ruins before 6:30. Muddy had lent me his watch, and it was that time when I started to draw the inscriptions on Stela 29. This was the only task that I had left for myself to do this morning, but I knew that it was going to take some time. The monument is an early one, and the glyphs are highly elaborated, with cross hatching, double lining, circles, and extra ornaments, all time consumers when it comes to drawing.

I was about half through when the shouts of the mulada advised they were getting under way. I looked at Muddy's watch; it was just 8:20. I recognized Chico's halloos and also the melancholy falsetto one that Alfred gives vent to in the bush. These gradually grew fainter as the mulada passed farther and farther on ahead. I worked on for more than an hour before finishing.

When I got back to camp, it was a changed place. In the trail coming into it was a tin of lunch—crackers and cheese—with a note from Rick saying they were getting under way at 8:15. Our animals were saddled, and we only waited long enough to tie on my bag of drawing materials, notebook, and measure. We left camp at 9:45 and five minutes later were riding behind the mounds on the east side of the city.

I bid fareweil to the ruins, as we left them behind. There has scarcely been a place on the face of the globe that I have wanted to see more for the past seven years than Piedras Negras. Our thirteen day stay here has been profitable beyond my greatest expectations. Five new monuments and three of them dated, besides a lot of new Secondary Series, and all the Supplementary Series. These, with Rutherford's photographic record and Ricketson's map, a fine piece of work, make a splendid rounding out of the field season.

Estanislas and I rode forward at a good gait. We stopped for ten minutes to eat lunch and then continued. The way seemed much shorter returning. It was still early in the afternoon when we passed Tres Champas and said goodbye to Petén for this season to enter Mexico again for the second time within three weeks.

1932

EXPLORATION OF CALAKMUL

Eleven years after the trip to Piedras Negras, each season seeing Morley traveling the breadth of the jungle realm continuously in quest of the precious date glyphs, word came of what appeared might be the greatest of all records of the ancient Maya chronology. In 1931 Cyrus L. Lundell, an American botanist in the employ of the Mexican Exploitation Company, encountered some extensive ruins in a remote district of eastern Campeche. After making a brief survey himself, he notified the Carnegie Institution of the ruins in the belief that the site was unknown to archaeologists. Morley agreed that another "lost city" had been found and was particularly intrigued with the prospects of exploration of Calakmul, as the newly found center was known, because of an adjacent logwood swamp by that name, because Lundell stated that an unusually large number of stelae appeared to have been erected there. Just four months later, when work in progress at Chichén Itzá permitted him to do so, Morley and several co-workers hurried south.

The site of Calakmul proved to have one hundred three stelae scattered throughout its plazas. Of these, seventy-three were sculptured. The total number was far greater than that known from any other Classic period center. Unfortunately, the large number of markers did not indicate an exceptionally long period of occupation but merely that the residents of Calakmul had raised more than one stela at various period-endings. Furthermore, none of the sculptures were of particular artistic merit. The emphasis had been on quantity and not on quality.

April 3, Sunday
We are off on another expedition, this time seven strong: Frances [Mrs. Morley], Karl Ruppert, John Bolles, Gustav Stromsvik, Tarsisio, Arturo, and me. But to go back to the beginning of the day.

We were almost packed. Day before yesterday most of our outfit had been shipped through direct to the Mexican Exploitation Company. This morning right after breakfast the remaining containers were assembled.

It was cool and a little dusty and the journey to Mérida, usually long at this time of year, seemed to pass swiftly. Karl is to be disbursing officer on this expedition, so I left him to make all arrangements in Mérida.

April 5, Tuesday

A frightfully long day, twenty hours from the time we rose at 4:00 until midnight when we retired, also a record from Mérida to San Dimas, where we slept.

But to begin the day at its long-ago beginning. We rose at 4:00 and by half-past four Alberto was serving breakfast in our room and the night watchman was taking down our baggage.

Fernando and John Germon both were on hand and for once there was no baggage trouble; everything was put on the train expeditiously and without argument.

Our train left at 5:30. Presently we were going at a good clip, almost thirty miles an hour at the top speeds toward Campeche. It was a delightful ride down, cool and fresh, and the five hours and twenty minutes passed quickly. Toward the end of the run we fortified ourselves at the station of Pomuch with the locally celebrated Pan de Pomuch, a kind of sponge cake which is not bad eating. At least, when one eats it going to Campeche, one is too all in to care, and it serves to tide one over until luncheon.

When we pulled into Campeche, a horde of porters descended upon us, but though I saw several old friends, I staved them off until Brydon should show up. But he did not come. Next I asked if any of the porters were Mr. Brydon's people and several said yes, a pious lie as it later turned out. I gave them our baggage.

Brydon and the immigration official met us at the station. The bill for our second express shipment was signed and turned over to the boy who was handling our baggage, and we all bundled into autos and drove up to Brydon's house. Curiously enough, this was just next door to Don Salustino Abreu's where we stopped a year ago when we were here.

The motor transport was to have arrived at 1:00 sharp, but by the time we were all aboard with our luggage and ready to leave it was just 2:00. We bid the Brydon family adios, and Frances and I got into the first car to lead the way. John, Karl, and Gustav followed in the second automobile and Tarsisio and Arturo in the large truck with the kyacks and boxes.

We passed an old hacienda named Victoria. Forty minutes out we reached the first village, China, where we waited for the truck, and waited and waited and waited.

Some school boys, none older than ten, were playing baseball with a stick for a bat and an egg-shaped ball made of string. We watched this game, encouraging its players, until school began, when they all disappeared.

It was 3:40 when the truck finally appeared. Manuel Hernandez, the owner and driver, said he broke a piece of the truck at the edge of Campeche and had to put back to get a spare part to replace it.

From China John, Karl, and Gustav took the lead, and we went into second place. At 4:10 we passed a small plantation called Xanchakan and at 4:45 another called Mokolchakan. After this we began to have serious trouble with our carburetor. Our driver, who was not a good mechanic though a good enough driver, began tinkering with it. When the truck came in, the two chauffeurs actually took the carburetor apart and cleaned it out. This lost us a precious half hour of daylight. When they got it together again, it missed even worse than before, if that were possible.

I decided that we would change over to the truck, leaving the auto to follow. Our personal baggage was put behind. We sat beside the driver, Manuel Hernandez, and thus proceeded.

At 5:30 we came to the edge of the savanna which was not as open as the great savannas of central Petén. Twenty minutes later we reached the ranch of San Nicolas where the boys had stopped their car and were eating oranges; in fact, they were eating a sort of supper. We pushed on ahead from here, still in the truck though our auto was following just behind, apparently again working all right.

As the sun was going down, we came to the village of Hol, where we stopped for five minutes to change back into the car, which was more comfortable riding than the truck. Although darkness fell swiftly, the stars gave sufficient light and at first we made out fairly well. From Hol to San Dimas is nine leagues. We hoped we might be in by 9:00 or 10:00, certainly by the latter.

After some stretches of savanna, the forest closed around us, and the road grew rapidly worse. There were stumps of trees a good eighteen inches high, rocks, bejucas, vines, and occasionally even fallen trees; it was dark and, in addition to the hazard of stones in the road on which to break an axle, there was the overhead hazard of being lacerated by thorny branches.

Another unpleasant feature was the ant hazard. The branches and boughs which occasionally brushed by us left these miserable pests on us. More than once we were severely stung in consequence.

About 9:00 our chauffeur drove us into a big stone which brought us to an immediate stop, killed the engine, bent the steering rod, and plunged Frances against the back of the front seat with such violence that she almost broke her nose. We stopped until the other cars came up. Then with a pole, chain, ropes, and the combined efforts of the six chauffeurs, the bent steering rod was bent back until it was straight and we proceeded on our way.

But this was not all. Sometime later our stupid chauffeur took a right hand road when the left hand one was clearly the better traveled. This was after we had crossed a small stream called the Paso de Tanco, which the chauffeurs said was only two leagues from San Dimas.

I urged him to turn back because this right fork grew worse and worse;

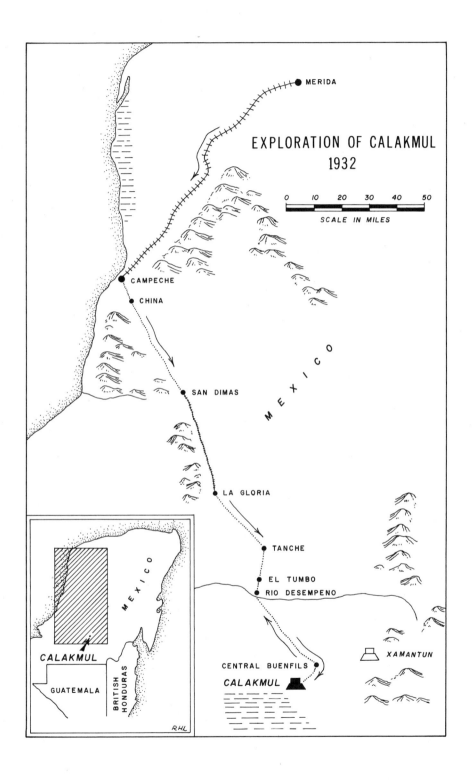

EXPLORATION OF CALAKMUL
1932

SCALE IN MILES

0   10   20   30   40   50

MERIDA

CAMPECHE

CHINA

SAN DIMAS

M E X I C O

LA GLORIA

TANCHE

EL TUMBO

RIO DESEMPENO

XAMANTUN

CENTRAL BUENFILS

CALAKMUL

CALAKMUL

M E X I C O

GUATEMALA

BRITISH HONDURAS

RHL

the fall of trees and vines more frequent and overgrown in every way. After about twenty minutes of this heavy going, we came to an impasse, a heavy fall of trees and vines, and he had to turn around. I had him examine his gasoline here to see how it was holding out. He had three inches left. We made our way back to the left fork. Although we could not see the traces of the other cars, this was the only way they could have gone. It was equally certain they were ahead because our costly mistake had delayed us more than half an hour.

About 10:00 we caught up to them, stopped because the front automobile had run into a stump and bent the front axle. Gustav reported this a really serious business, but they got out the pole, chain, and ropes again, and again bent it back into shape, and we proceeded. This time the boys were first, the truck second, and our car last.

We drove along this way for another half an hour, finally reaching San Dimas at 11:00 sharp. Cue Sánchez, the administrador of the place, met us. The truck and autos were quickly unloaded. The boys elected to sleep near the garage where the cars had stopped, but Sánchez said there were rooms and supper waiting for all of us up at the Casa Principal, which we could see on the top of a hill. The boys, however, were too tired to care to eat, so they hung their hammocks in the house next to the garage and went to sleep at once. We waited only until Tarsisio and Arturo could get out Frances's hammock, my cot, and our bedding. Then Sánchez took us up the hill.

We had a large corner room, screened in but with no furniture other than two chairs. It had a very high ceiling, and the ventilation was good. It was just 12:00 midnight when we got into bed, twenty hours exactly since rising.

April 6, Wednesday

We rose about 7:00. Tarsisio and Arturo had already been down to waken Karl, John, and Gustav. They reported that our first big shipment of baggage left before daylight this morning on two platforms. We were to see more of these platforms ourselves before the day was over.

We sat down to a delicious breakfast of eggs, chocolate, tortillas, black beans, and chicken cooked with small tomatoes and onions. After bidding Mrs. Sánchez goodbye and congratulating the cook on the triumph of her chicken dish, cementing the congratulations with something more substantial than words, we went down the hill to the San Dimas office. All the remaining baggage had been piled on three platforms, on the last of which a seat with a canvas back had been fixed for Frances and me. These platforms are cars about three meters long with eight wheels. They are drawn by two mules tandem, fastened to the car by a single pair of traces and driven without reins of any kind. The driver sits on the front end of the truck with a pole in one hand with which he not only breaks the car but also actually steers it by pushing on the ground from one side to the other as need arises.

We pulled out with a great flourish of whips and shouting. At first the mules were peppy, dashing along perhaps as fast as eight miles per hour, but out on the road they soon lost this pep. I imagine we averaged a little over two leagues an hour, maybe five and a half miles.

The first lap of our journey was to the station of Yacasay, which we did in one and three-quarters hours from San Dimas. There we waited while the drivers changed mules and had their lunches. In the next stretch to Yahaltun we had to stop several times to unload platforms coming toward us so that they could be tilted off the tracks in order to let us pass.

Beyond Yahaltun we ran through a great milpa fire, almost in the midst of which we had to stop to load some bundles of ramon leaves on the first platform.

Just before reaching Hidalgo we came to a rather sharp small descent known as El Cerro del Cura from the fact that a number of years ago a platform carrying a priest and his impedimenta got away from the driver, dashed down hill, ran off the tracks and threw the priest and his luggage off to one side, the latter on top of the former, breaking his neck.

Beyond Hidalgo we passed a life boat of a size capable of holding twenty-four people. Gustav was sleeping when the second car drew past it, and Karl and John wakened him. When Gustav saw that boat, he said he thought he was still asleep. Ramon told us that all through this section in the rainy season, especially in October, the water rises several meters. The track is completely submerged at that time and the only traffic through here is by boat.

We reached La Gloria at 4:30. I looked up the administrador and presented my letter to him. He was expecting me, but the truck of Mr. Buenfils, the only one working on this stretch of the road between La Gloria and the Rio Desempeño, had left for the river about two or three hours before we got in.

This was a bit of sourness, but as a truck from Tuxpena drove in at that time, I tried to persuade the driver to take us on. He said, however, that he could not stop his run. So that was that.

The Buenfils truck is expected back any time between 9:00 tomorrow morning and 9:00 tomorrow night. It left here at 2:00 in the afternoon and the trip usually takes twenty-four hours, but may take much more if (1) it rains and (2) if they have a breakdown, which latter happens not infrequently.

The situation ahead of us seems to be this: from here to Tanche is ten leagues and from there to the Río Desempeño, eight leagues, the really bad part being the two or three leagues this side of the river. Here it may be necessary to transfer baggage to carts for the last three leagues to the river and from there to take another truck for the remaining eleven leagues to Central Buenfils. It all depends on the return of the truck, and on that not overly certain fact we have to wait.

La Gloria is a hideous misnomer. There are about a dozen houses of thatch and corrugated iron, many dogs, chickens, pigs, and more fleas.

April 7, Thursday

All hands aboard on the truck which arrived after lunch. Frances and I sat forward; Gustav braced horizontally across the truck; Karl and John in the hold amidships; our two orientals with two natives aft, where there was much movement. The car was cranked and began to throb and tremble mightily. With shouts and adioses, there was a great snorting, and we began to lurch forward.

We turned south out of the settlement and got perhaps two blocks when we heaved forward into a deep hole in the road and something under the hood broke. A hasty investigation revealed that it was the valve spring. The men searched through a tool box which contained everything under the sun, even a sour orange, but no valve spring.

While we were thus held up, another roaring approached. It was the White truck from Tuxpena, which I had tried to hire yesterday. The driver stopped, got out, and began to help. They sent back to La Gloria for an extra spring while we sat and waited in the broiling sun. Karl suggested bridge and produced a deck of cards. A precarious table was built of my notebook case and a camera case. We played two complete rubbers and were well on the third when the valve was replaced after several trips back to La Gloria. This breakdown cost us just two hours.

Such a road ahead! A wide swath of the forest had been cut so as to let the sun dry out the mud. Down this we careened and cavorted, sometimes making as much as fifteen miles an hour. The clearing made the overhead hazard almost negligible at first but later this became dangerous.

After an hour and three-quarters we came to the crest of a really high limestone ridge, called here Cerro del Palomo Blanco. The grade was steep and the road rocky. I judged we had gone up almost one hundred meters before we reached the summit. Twenty-five minutes beyond we came to the village of Paso Hol, where we stopped to pick some sour oranges. This village has a tiny church, the masonry of which looks almost colonial. The whole church cannot have been more than twelve by fifteen feet inside, but it was a definite church with its bell tower in front. The men and women here looked distinctly Maya in character. There was no mistaking them for anything else. Since beyond to Petén lies only forest with an occasional chicle camp, I felt this village must be the outpost in this direction of the Yucatecan Maya.

Tanche was reached just as the last of the daylight was fading from the sky. Here we made a long stop. The station was in the charge of Don Pancho Buenfils's brother, whom I saluted with respect. I asked him if we could cook our supper, and he very graciously assented. Our chauffeur and his three assistants fueled, oiled, and watered the car. After an hour we continued on our way, the last lap of the day, a stretch of five leagues to El Tumbo at the edge of the akalche on the north side of the Río Desempeño.

The night was absolutely cloudless. The stars were brilliant points of light that flashed through the trees. We all shook down into our places in the bottom of the truck and for a final two and a half hours lurched back and forth over the road. The trees were now very thick overhead, and there was danger of being hurt by being struck by a branch. After an hour, we overtook a cart drawn by five mules, which we could not pass because of the narrowness of the road. We were behind this for another hour until we finally came to a place where the teamster could draw to one side. Then we forged ahead to Tumbo.

April 8, Friday

I had told Tarsisio to waken us all at 4:30, but it was after 5:00 by the watch when I was called. We got up in the cold and began packing, folding up my cot, taking down pabellones and hammocks, and stowing away baggage. It was decided that breakfast should be short so that we could push on to El Río as speedily as possible. We washed out of the tin in which the boys carry extra water for the White truck and stood up to breakfast of fried eggs, bacon, tea and crackers.

If the road up to this point had been bad, beyond it was impossible. Although drying out under the suns of the last week, the akalche was still damp and the mud in places the consistency of clay. Logs had to be chained to the rear wheels. With this we made some shift, but it was hard slogging.

It is called two leagues to El Río Desempeño from Tumbo, mostly akalche. It took us from 7:00 to 10:00 to do this bit. The truck bogged down in the thick dry mud and repeatedly had to be helped out with stout poles which were almost logs, chained to the rear wheels.

About midway of the akalche, we saw a truck coming toward us. It was another White similarly served by a half dozen men helping it through the soft spots. When this drew nearer, our boys said that Señor Osorno was with it. I introduced myself and gave him my letter. He knew we were coming south, so he had come out to look for us. With some maneuvering we got by the second truck and, with Señor Osorno driving, we managed to get into El Río Desempeño. The aguada through which we came is now a kilometer in length, and they even have boats on it.

After a hearty lunch at El Río Desempeño, we continued on our way, and what was to follow was unspeakable. It should be noted, to begin with, that the truck is not fitted with any type of tire other than hard rubber, and the road is only a cleared right of way with the trees cut down and the stumps removed. The distance is about forty-four kilometers between El Río and Central Buenfils. It was 11:55 when we left the former, and it was 6:10 when we reached the latter.

The forest seemed to be definitely higher over this last stretch and the road more hilly, though we had several blistering akalches to cross. Fortunately they were not wet but were rough. The White truck lurched and jerked, careened and cavorted, jumped and jolted. It was absolutely necessary to hold oneself rigidly braced since otherwise one could easily have broken a neck or back by being thrown against the sides of the truck. It was almost as bad as riding in a volancoche, but every muscle of arm and back and neck took a terrible beating. When we finally reached our destination, we were all sore as though we had been beaten with sticks.

April 9, Saturday

Our mulada quickly passed out of the enormous clearing around Central Buenfils and plunged into the high bush. As we rode along, we noticed the absence of all corozo palm and escoba palm. In fact, there was almost no palm at all anywhere except the small, rather scrubby variety which we have in tins in front of our house at Chichén Itzá. According to Lundell, the distance from Central Buenfils to Calakmul is four leagues. It took us just three hours.

We began passing small outlying groups of mounds some distance out, perhaps little suburban centers all belonging to the great ceremonial center we were about to visit. A little before 11:30 we passed the aguada of Calakmul on the right. The main plaza lay a kilometer beyond. We had decided to have our laborers camp at the aguada, but we were to live in the main plaza. The baggage was strewn around under the trees in a semi-cleared area which I assume had been Lundell's camp. There was a lean-to of poles here, and the area had a general appearance of having been occupied not more than three or four months before.

The east side of the main plaza of Calakmul is formed by a single long mound from which originally rose three different buildings, the middle one being the highest. This must have been a noble building, or triple building, in its day, and though comparatively low as the buildings here go, it must have been one of the most effective from an architectural point of view. In front of it originally had stood no less than fifteen stelae. The one which drew my attention first was the small Stela 9 which Lundell had photographed and which is made of a sort of slate, a very unusual material. I had dated this provisionally at 9.18.10.0.0 [A.D. 800] by a Period Ending date on the front from one of Lundell's photographs. But while I was studying this just after lunch today, I found an Initial Series on the right side about half way down, and later on the left side at the top I found another. This is a very unusual feature, but not unique. I think I have reported fourteen or fifteen others elsewhere. The inscription on the left side has all the five period glyphs and the Initial Series introducing glyph fairly well preserved, although they are carved in a delicate incised line. This number reads 9.10.16.16.19 3 *Cauac* 2 *Mac* [A.D. 647]. The other side is not so clear and will need some calculations to bring it into line.

After a long hard day the laborers were told to go to their camp at 6:00. About 7:00 we sat down to a good dinner, very hungry and tired but well satisfied with the day. After dinner everybody retired to his pabellon. Real work starts tomorrow.

April 10, Sunday

What an incredible day! As old Dr. Woodward used to say, "It would have been incredible if it had not have happened." Twenty-two new stelae in addition to Lundell's sixty-three and thirty Initial Series were found. But to go back to the very beginning.

We decided to follow the sequence of stelae worked out by Lundell. We turned our attention first to No. 1, just to the left of the trail coming in. This is standing but in poor condition. It seems to have an Initial Series. Stelae 2, 3, 4, and 5 are standing, but No. 6 is fallen. All appear to be plain. Stela 7 also seems to be plain but Stela 8 yielded our second Initial Series. I first read this as 9.14.10.0.0 [A.D. 721]. On Stela 9 I had picked up two Initial Series yesterday, making a total of four up to now.

At this point, we climbed the high middle building of the triple structure D and looked for Lundell's Stela 10. This proved to be a plain square altar rather than a stela, so we omitted his No. 10 from the list of stelae.

Stelae 10, 11, and 12 were plain. Stela 13 standing on the plaza level proved to be sculptured but was in such bad condition that I could do nothing with it. Stela 14 was even more doubtful. Stela 15 is an enormous slab nearly twelve feet high, fallen on its face. This is a job for Gustav and is a big one. How many tons it weighs we can only guess, perhaps six or eight. Stela 16 is standing and yielded our fifth Initial Series, 9.19.0.0.0 [A.D. 810].

Stela 17 is a very small stela less than two meters high sculptured with a figure on the front and glyphs on the sides, but I could detect no dates. Stela 18 seems to have been only a fragment from the top of some monument, though it had originally been carved with glyphs.

On the three stelae, numbers 19, 20, and 21, in front of the south end of the triple structure D, the first and the last only were carved, and neither yielded a date.

This finished the monuments in the main plaza, or rather on its east side, and we crossed to structure F on its west side, in front of which are three stelae, No. 22 below and Nos. 23 and 24 above. The first is very probably plain, but the two above are both sculptured. I think Stela 23 records the Initial Series 9.13.10.0.0 [A.D. 702] and Stela 24 the next lahuntun ending also as an Initial Series, 9.13.10.0.0 , the sixth and seventh Initial Series.

Behind this same structure are three more stelae, Nos. 25, 26, and 27. The first two surely record Initial Series, the eighth and ninth, the former 9.15.10.0.0. [A.D. 741] and the latter 9.15.5.0.0 [A.D. 736]. I feel strongly that Stela 27 which is still standing must have recorded the date 9.15.0.0.0 [A.D. 731] but I could not prove this.

John, who had gradually worked on ahead of Karl, Gus, and me, presently called out that he had found some new stelae west of structure I. We crossed the court behind F and found Stelae 59 and 60. The former is fallen, the latter standing. Both are carved, though in this preliminary inspection I got dates from neither. Behind, we came to John's two new monuments just west of structure I. Stela 61 was carved though fallen. I got no date here. Stela 62 may have had the end of katun 16 on it, but I got no Initial Series from this stela.

Stelae 63, 64, and 65 on this outer side of the same court were all down. The first and last are very small and probably plain; the middle one has an Initial Series, the tenth, which I read then as 9.14.0.0.0 [A.D. 711].

Still following John's voice, we turned north here, and passing around the west end of structure L, joined him near the high pyramid M, where he had discovered the sixth new monument, Stela 56. It was in very poor condition, and we could not tell whether it had been sculptured or not. Stela 57 (fallen) and Stela 58 (standing) both yielded Initial Series, the eleventh and twelfth, which recorded the same date, 9.17.0.0.0 [A.D. 771].

From here we turned south, passing between the walls of John's newly discovered ball court (structure K) at the northern end of which we found a small sculptured stone which we called Stela 66. Passing out of the south end of this court, we soon picked up Stelae 67, 68, and 69, the last new and all three fallen. Stela 67 yielded our thirteenth Initial Series, which I read as 9.18.10.0.0 [A.D. 800].

Rounding the northeast corner of structure P, we came on the great row of five standing stelae, numbers 70-74. All five had Initial Series, bringing our total of Initial Series up to eighteen. I could not read all of them out of hand, so to speak. Stelae 71 and 73 record 9.14.0.0.0 [A.D. 711] and Stela 74 perhaps 9.13.0.0.0 [A.D. 692]. Stelae 70 and 72 I could not get in this first hurried survey, but I hope to read them before I leave.

From here, we passed east and picked up a new monument, Stela 80, in front of structure 0. This has an Initial Series 9.18.0.0.0 [A.D. 790], our nineteenth so far. It is standing. We proceeded east from Stela 80, hitting the trail going back to camp, and stopped at structure E long enough only to locate it. Then we came in to luncheon, highly elated with our morning's adventure.

After dinner we went to structure E and picked up Stelae 28 and 29, both standing, both carved and both partly buried. Both also had Initial Series, the twentieth and twenty-first, and one, Stela 28, seemed to record a katun 10 date and the other, Stela 29, a katun 9 date.

Going around to the opposite side of this same mound above on the terrace, we picked up Stelae 30 and 31, both fallen and in bad condition.

The six large stelae Nos. 32-37 seem to have been sculptured with columns of glyphs on their backs as well as on their two sides. Of these, the only two I could be sure had Initial Series were Stelae 35 and 36, the twenty-second and twenty-third Initial Series. Both seem to record dates in katun 11, though I could decipher neither exactly.

Just before lunch, Victor Audinette, the Belizano laborer, in working northward from structure 0 and Stela 80, had found four monuments which seemed to be new. So after finishing with structure E, we went off to the west and eventually relocated them. Instead of four, there are five. All are standing except the second from the left. The great surprise was to find that the five large standing monuments (Stelae 75-79) are actually on the west side of the same plaza as Victor Audinette's five newly discovered monuments. The inscriptions on all of these are badly effaced. I was able to tell that three at least had Initial Series on them.

We next moved over to structure B on the east side of the trail. This is the highest building in the city and cannot be far from one hundred fifty feet in height. From its northwest corner a diagonal platform runs out near which are two fallen stelae. On one was our twenty-seventh new Initial Series. The carving is fine and the Initial Series which reads 9.4.0.0.0 [A.D. 514] must be brought forward by later Secondary Series to a much later date.

While I was looking at this, Karl had climbed the pyramid himself, which he describes as having two stages on the north side. After having reached the first summit, he found he had to descend and then climb again to the final highest summit. When he came down, he was exhausted and dripping with sweat. He kidded Gustav into going up it and the latter reported a high sharp pyramid to the southwest on the horizon, which must be the site Lundell says Shufeldt discovered back in 1914.

After the several excursions, we gathered our belongings together, descended from Stela 43 and pushed east looking for structure A. On our way we passed a long plain shaft to which we gave the number 47 and then came on Lundell's great round altar which is ten feet in diameter. This was plain but the biggest round stone I have ever seen.

Stela 52, the most beautiful standing stone at Calakmul, could be seen through the trees. This is a great shaft nearly four meters high and well over a meter in width, sculptured on its front with a figure facing to the observer's left and on the sides with glyphs. The left side has an Initial Series 9.15.0.0.0 [A.D. 731], the twenty-eighth thus far. The glyphs are the most beautiful I have seen anywhere in the city. There are one or two Secondary Series which I cannot connect at the moment, but these will come on closer study.

From structure A we struck off to the northeast through the bush to the large standing structure. No monuments were associated with this, but what a monstrous building. Some of the rooms were still preserved and the record of previous visitors was scratched on the wall. The earliest was in 1926, but to Lundell, who was here on December 29 through 31 of last year (1931) should go the credit of discovery, since it was he who first brought it to the attention of the outside world.

And what a man. All day long he tramped through this bush with his map in hand to make it easy for us. We have checked him almost pace by pace and every time found him right. We have every convenience for camp comfort, a half a dozen men besides ourselves to cut the bush, and I suspect he had very little comfort. He did a splendid thing, and I deeply appreciate his fine spirit of generosity and love of scientific truth which prompted him to call this matter to the Institution's attention. I know we can do this great site justice, and we will see that he gets credit for his discovery.

But it was getting late, and we still had one more of his monuments to see, one standing by itself some two hundred yards northeast of structure D. With Jesus as our guide, we came back through camp and then struck northeast from structure D. We walked for quite a distance and finally came to a mound with two fallen stelae on its south side. This could not be Lundell's last monument because that is still standing on the west side of a mound, whereas the two just found are both fallen on the south side of a mound.

These are Stelae 83 and 84. Both are new, bringing our total of new monuments for the day up to twenty-two. This makes a total of eighty-five stelae for the site.

It was now getting on to 5:00, and we were all ready to call it a day. But what a day! Twenty-two new stelae, thirty-one new Initial Series, and a grand total of more stelae than any other Maya site yet reported, probably more than any other Maya site in existence. And there are probably more stelae to be picked up when we have covered this whole central area. We are already speculating on the possibility of finding around one hundred.

We came back to camp and took much needed sponge baths and then had supper.

April 11, Monday

Today was the first day of detailed work at Calakmul. As indicated in the foregoing pages, yesterday we gave the site a bird's eye view, but today we settled down to business.

Including Jesus Garcia, who is foreman, we had eight men. They are all good men, and with them John set off cutting his lines through the bush. Karl and I had nobody as yet, but when the Rio Desempeño bunch get in, we ought to draw one. I stayed close to Gustav, however, who had Alberto, Jesus, and the boy Demetrio. José Carmen, our youngest boy, stayed around camp to fetch water.

I started with Stela 1. This surely has an Initial Series. I could not read it, however. It looks like 9.10.0.?.5 but the original is too far gone to permit anything like exact decipherment.

Before lunch Jesus, in exploring the northeast section of the city looking for the last of Lundell's monuments, had found five, six, or seven stelae; he didn't know which. So after we had eaten, Karl, Gustav, and I went looking for these stelae. First we followed along the trail clear back to the boys' camp at the aguada where Laborio's señora, a dog, and two horses were holding down that place. Here we turned off into the bush to the right and continued for quite a time, passing another aguada on our right. Finally, climbing a slight rise and passing several mounds, we came on to a plaza with nine more stelae! These were arranged on the two sides of a plaza, five fallen on the east side and four still standing on the north side. At first it seemed that all nine were plain, but on digging under Stela 87, it alone seems to be sculptured on its under face. The others, however, are plain.

On returning to camp, Gustav began to turn the enormous Stela 15. While he was doing this, John found two more very small stelae out in the main plaza about midway between the kitchen and their own tent cover. These were given the numbers 85 and 86. The latter is sculptured with a very interesting figure on the front and curious square glyphs on its two sides; the back is plain. The glyphs each seem to be separated by three dots each, almost like the glyphs on pottery.

Karl returned about this time and reported three more new stelae, numbers 96, 97, and 98. Number 97 has an Initial Series, so that our total score is now thirty-two.

Meanwhile Gustav continued to try to raise Stela 15. At first he thought the front of the stela had no glyphs on it, but when it was nearly raised, Frances distinguished three glyphs in the upper left corner, the first of which has a coefficient of 9. This is preceded by the familiar torch-like prefix that sometimes accompanies the days of Period Ending dates. This is followed very clearly by an 18 *Mol.* The whole date therefore reads 9.19.0.0.0 9 *Ahau* 18 *Mol* [A.D. 810], or a repetition as a Period Ending of the Initial Series recorded on the nearby Stela 16. This gives us another date.

Just before quitting today, we tried to push this monument upright, but no use. It was decided to wait until tomorrow morning for the final push.

We were needing a number of things in camp. Gustav wanted more axes, shovels, and picks, and also twenty-five meters of half-inch rope. Frances wanted tortillas, eggs, a chicken, and some sugar for cooking. I wrote a note to Don Ambrosio, asking him to send these things out tomorrow by young José Carmen who will ride over on Victor Audinette's white horse, bringing the things back on it.

April 12, Tuesday

We were one man short today in consequence of José Carmen's going to Central Buenfils. The first thing after breakfast Gustav's cuadrilla, with the help of John's, tried to give Stela 16 a final shove that would have put it back straight. Push as they would, the dead weight of its eight tons proved too much for them, and Gustav had to finish the job with his two jacks, just as he had begun it.

When this was finished, we moved down to the south side of the main plaza where Stelae 28 and 29 are standing almost buried in the fall of debris from the top of the building behind them. I saw that work on these stelae was going to take some time, so I was going to examine and prepare for photography those monuments associated with the structure of the west side of the main plaza. I picked up Frances in camp, and we climbed this mound. As we looked over some stelae which I had hurriedly viewed yesterday, I discovered an Initial Series which I had missed earlier. This was on

Stela 27 and was our thirty-third Initial Series. It read 9.15.10.0.0 [A.D. 741], the same date as on Stela 25 on the other side of Stela 26.

About this time we heard John shouting somewhere to the northwest. Finally he called that he had a new stela and something even more important. We made our way through the forest toward his voice, until presently it developed he was over by the mound he calls the Castillo. This has three stelae on the east side. John's new stela was on the south side of this. It is fallen and sculptured with glyphs on the sides. I could find neither an Initial Series nor even a date. This is Stela 99. If we could locate Lundell's standing monument in the northeast section, we could round out an even hundred. We will surely find a Stela 100 before we are finished.

John next directed us to the end of the line he was then bushing. We were to follow it west and when it stopped to look around on the ground. We walked out this and finally came to the end. To the left of the line a piece of the native limestone was outcropping and on this was carved a human head in very deep relief. It was in a fine state of preservation in spite of the fact that it had been exposed at the ground level where it was most subject to the attacks of humic acid. John left us the discovery of this interesting carving. We exposed a section of the outcrop nine and a half feet high and seven and a half feet wide. On this was an enormous kneeling captive with arms bound behind his back. The figure is nude and shows his genitalia very prominently. Behind and above is another smaller captive figure, the face of which has flaked away. There is a third figure, much smaller, sitting behind the larger figure. On another piece of the limestone there is a further carving, but this continues under a tree. It will require considerable work to trace it in this direction.

We worked here, sweating and brushing until we had uncovered the above mentioned section from roots and encumbered earth. If we can only get a good photograph of this carving, it will create a great sensation at home. We knocked off at 11:00 and came down John's line until we found his transit. Then with Juan Andres as a guide, we struck eastward until we hit the trail and thence went south to our camp.

After luncheon I went to see Gústav's work. I had not been able to get the date of Stela 29 up to this point, but now the light was better on its west side. I saw that the katun coefficient which I had been misreading as 10 is 9. This gave me 9.9.?.0.0. I looked at the tun and it seemed to be more like 10 than anything else. This agreed with the month's coefficient of 13, i.e. 9.9.10.0.0 2 *Ahau* 13 *Pop* [A.D. 623]. I next examined the month itself and was able to pick out the kin element and the knot element; indeed there can be no doubt that the month is 13 *Pop*.

From here we went over to structure F on the west side of the main plaza. There was no work to be done on Stela 22 which is little more than a pile of fallen stone, crumbling into dust. Of the two stelae above, numbers 23 and 24, both present the same Initial Series 9.13.10.0.0 7 *Ahau* 3 *Cumhu*

[A.D. 702]. The former is standing, the latter fallen. Stela 23 is made of a very poor quality of stone, and even though standing, the relief is practically gone. On the left side at the bottom is a nodule of flint, which the stone tools of the ancient masons or sculptors could not remove or even reduce in size.

On the front at the top there is a large hole which must have been filled with limestone and mortar in ancient times. Gustav worked on Stela 24, turning its principal fragments. There was little left on the under side.

I was writing my diary in camp when José Carmen got back from Central Buenfils. He brought all the things I asked for including a chicken which he tied to a tree. It escaped soon, and he had quite a chase around the main plaza, the hen clucking madly, until finally Frances joined the chase. Between the two of them, they cornered her finally, and José Carmen brought the hen back into captivity.

April 13, Wednesday
Another day, and Gustav and I are getting on with our end of this job. We first went to Stela 24, which Gustav finished turning, and then continued on over behind this same mound which is structure F. Karl and I paced off the top of this structure, which must be at least thirty-five feet high and one hundred feet square on top. The only construction is the low mound or platform which was just west of Stelae 23 and 24.

Having finished with the monuments in this group, we moved our men over to Stelae 63, 64, and 65. The first of these proved a dud. It was a small slab of stone but very hard. We had high hopes that the figure on the under side would be beautifully preserved but to our disgust there was nothing on the under side. Stela 64 I had originally read as 9.14.0.0.0 declared by an Initial Series on its left side, but a closer examination this afternoon showed that the katun coefficient had been 19 instead of 14, i.e. four dots and three bars instead of four dots and two bars.

This corrected reading was further confirmed by finding the day of the terminal date of the corrected reading as 9.19.0.0.0 9 *Ahau* 18 *Mol* [A.D. 810]. This is the latest date yet found here but is also recorded on Stelae 15 and 16 in the main plaza.

I expected Stela 65 to be plain like Stela 63. It was small and appeared to be a sister monument, that is two plain ones flanking a sculptured one. To our delight, however, after Gustav had turned it, there was a beautifully carved figure holding a manikin scepter in her right hand and a little shield in its left hand. But not a glyph on it. The sides were plain, as also the back, and not a single glyph on the front. Secondary lime deposits, including many snail shells, covered the front, but with care these may be removed. We ought to get an excellent picture of this little gem.

After setting Stela 65 on its edge, we left this court with structure I on its east, structure J on its south, structure L on its north and the ball court K on its west side, and moved our men to the row of three stelae — Nos. 67-69— just north of structure F.

The last of these does not appear on Lundell's map. It is almost completely buried, and Gustav put Jesus to digging out its left side. To my great delight an Initial Series developed here presently, making the thirty-fourth here so far. I was able to decipher this without much difficulty as 9.18.10.0.0 10 *Ahau* 8 *Zac* [A.D. 800]. So the day was fairly successful for me after all.

April 15, Friday

Three new monuments were discovered late this afternoon, bringing the total up to one hundred three, of which we have found forty and Lundell sixty-three. One of these, found by Karl, on the very summit of structure A has an Initial Series, our thirty-sixth. It is hard to see how Lundell missed it, though it is fallen forward on its face. Karl reports it as 9.15.0.0.9 [A.D. 731]. The glyphs are beautiful. This will be given the number 89. Coming back to camp, John said he had found two new stelae, both small, in the main plaza. I could hardly believe it. One was hardly fifty feet from our dining room and the other no more than seventy-five.

April 16, Saturday

About 3:30 Gustav and I decided to go over to structure A and climb it to see Karl's new stela, No. 89. We left his men digging in front of Stela 43 and fought our way through the thick bush just east of structure B until we ran into a line running south past the southeast corner of structure B when it ran into another bearing generally east. We followed this until it reached structure A, which we began to climb.

This pyramid goes up very steeply, and if it were not for the trees and saplings which grow on its sides, would be extremely difficult to climb. As we approached the top, we seemed to come into a different ecological zone altogether. The big trees disappeared, and wild henequen, thorny bush, and even a chacté quite reminiscent of Chichén Itzá, were about us. This sparser growth is undoubtedly due to the fact that there is little water held in the steep upper part of this pyramid and the plant life is more characteristic of our Yucatán flora than it is of the heavier rain forest growth on the ground level here.

Forest, trees, bush everywhere and not a clearing, much less a habitation, in sight. Depressing it was. A rain storm was in progress to the southwest, and in this direction one could see where the high forest broke and the big akalche everyone speaks of lies.

After looking around a little, we came down to the stela which lies on its face. On the left side is an Initial Series which apparently records the date 9.15.0.0.14 5 *Ix* 7 *Zac*. At the top of the right side is an inverted *Ahau* with three dots above it. On stela C at Quirigua and on lintels 2 and 3 at Piedras Negras the inverted *Ahau* is a substantive for the kin sign and if three kins is added to 5 *Ix* 7 *Zac,* the date 8 *Caban* 10 *Zac* is reached. The monument has 7 *Caban* 10 *Zac* which is probably an error in the original for 8 *Caban.* It will be quite delicate turning this over as it lies on the slope. Gustav says he can achieve it, and if he says he can, he will.

April 18, Monday

This morning Gustav and I worked at structure A. Six of the nine stelae there seem to have been dedicated in 9.15.0.0.0 [A.D. 731]. They are carved on unusually hard limestone for this site and beyond doubt are the finest stelae in the city. It is as though some master had carved them all.

Work was begun on Stelae 51 and 52. The former had fallen forward on its face but the magnificent sculpturing of the glyphs on the sides gave promise of something exceptional below. Stela 52 was standing but a great tree growing behind it had thrown roots around the base and these roots had to be cut out.

While some of Gustav's men were digging along the sides of Stela 51 getting it ready to turn this afternoon, others were digging around Stela 53, the sides of which were plain. This also had fallen face forward and Gustav was very doubtful about its having sculpturing on the under side. But this time he was mistaken.

It was not large, but the relief was magnificent. The figure holds a spear in its right hand and in his left a small round shield which has cross bands across it. The carving is beautiful, and altogether we are greatly pleased. The shaft is broken off at the level of the knees, and Lino Paat was put to work excavating just behind this upper part to see if he could locate the lower part of the shaft which must carry the feet of this figure.

In the meantime our two axmen were making a great well of light in the forest. The pictures we will take here are to be afternoon ones. It is a great patch of blue sky closed in by forest on all sides.

Stela 50 has a figure on it facing to the observer's left but very much cruder than the five beautiful stelae behind it. At first I thought the figure was sitting but in the end came to the conclusion it was standing. The waist is greatly constricted though a bar passes just below the waist which reached almost across the shaft. One point that was a special interest in connection with this small monument was the red paint which still adhered to it in many places. This was not the usual dark maroon red but a lighter brighter red. It must have been a lovely color when it was fresh.

In the afternoon with the moving picture camera Karl, his two men, Frances, José, Garcia, Gustav and I repaired to structure A where the turning of Stela 51 was gotten under way. From the first this monument proved troublesome. To begin with, it is an enormous shaft of stone thirteen feet long, five feet wide, and a foot and two inches thick. To be sure Gustav has raised larger stelae but the earth under this one was so soft that neither the jacks nor the rocks upon which they rested could get a good firm purchase below. Gradually he got it up bit by bit until it was inclined about seventy degrees with the horizontal. At this point, by assembling all hands, he tried to get it up the remaining twenty degrees by all pushing it at once, but it never budged.

While he was getting ready his next device, which involved the use of a pole some twenty-five feet long, we examined the relief. It is a beauty, the best we have found so far. The nose of the figure is slightly damaged, but the details of the carving are exquisite. Frances noticed an elaborate curling of the hair almost like an Egyptian wig. The glyphs are in fine condition.

It was too dangerous looking under this great slab, resting as it was on the jacks and a few slender poles, so we decided to wait a few minutes longer when it would be erect. Karl had taken movies of the various steps and had saved about fifteen feet for the final cleaned slab.

Gustav's plan was a good one. A great pole twenty-five feet long was raised against the under side of the stela; this pole was fitted into a heavy forked piece of wood, which was backed against a stump. The forked piece of wood served to keep the butt of the pole from slipping either way. A cable was tied to the upper end of the pole and then the force pulled on the cable. Slowly the stela rose until it was vertical and resting easily against a stout short pole, which had been provided to keep it from going all the way over. It was just right, and then an ugly thing happened.

When the crew at the end of the cable saw that the stela was up, they let the rope go slack. The pole tottered and then crashed to the ground parallel with the stela, knocking out the three props on the left side. There before our eyes two hours' arduous labor in the boiling sun went instantly for naught. The monument toppled over on its face again. That was that.

It was a great disappointment for us all. For one minute we saw the sculpture in the magnificent slanting light and then it was gone.

April 20, Wednesday

Frances found our forty-fifth Initial Series yesterday on Stela 48. The Initial Series is on the right side and reads 9.15.0.0.0 [A.D. 731]. It seemed that the sculpture on the front or exposed upper surface has entirely flaked off. I thought that it might be worthwhile to turn this monument over to see if there had been a design on the back or down the side. This monument had broken in three pieces, and Gustav turned his attentions to the middle piece first.

In order to turn this fragment over, it was necessary to bring down a dead limb of a tree. When this was felled, it was found to harbor a veritable metropolis of tree ants. All the rest of the time we were working on this monument, we were covered with these pests.

There is some evidence that Stela 48 had never been finished. In the first place, the inscription on the left side seems to be incomplete. Only the first five or six glyph blocks are carved. In the second place, there are two glyphs in the upper left corner on the front which have had the panel prepared for them but which have never been carved. The relief is so low as to be little more than incised. The right hand is extended down in front of the body as though the figure were sowing corn. The other hand is in much the same position. The fingers are noticeably elongated on both hands.

April 21, Thursday

Many surprises today including five new Initial Series, bringing our total up to a round fifty.

After breakfast we went first to the two stelae in front of structure Q which are now Stelae 93 and 94. The latter I had identified as an Initial Series on our original tour of inspection a week ago. This records the date 9.12.10.0.0 [A.D. 682]. I had given up the companion monument, Stela 93, but in order to make sure this morning I set two boys clearing along the two sides.

The right side was exposed first and this showed a line of two or three glyphs across the top of the monument and a figure facing to the observer's left below them. The left side was more promising. There had been an Initial Series here, the introducing glyph of which had disappeared all but the lower left corner.

April 22, Friday

John's work is over and Karl's practically so. We decided this morning that tomorrow they will go into Central Buenfils a day early and go on to a ruin six leagues beyond there, which Laborio knows and says there are two or three sculptured stelae there. To this end, I sent Jesus into Central Buenfils to bring back an arria of mules. He and Laborio will leave here tomorrow morning with Karl and John.

Jesus was despatched immediately after lunch to fetch the arria of five mules. Immediately after he had left, I went over to Stela 35 and think I read the Initial Series on its left side, the second on the monument, as 9.11.8.10.8 [A.D. 660]. The introducing glyph irregularly for this site occupies the space of one glyph block. The light was so good that I sent Genero back for Frances and the camera.

While Frances was photographing Stela 35 and later Stela 36, I took notes on the latter. This dates surely from katun 11, and probably tun 10 of that katun. The variable central element of the Initial Series introducing glyph is the moon sign. I think this Initial Series reads 9.11.10.0.0 11 *Ahau* 18 *Chen* [A.D. 662].

From here, in the white heat of about 1:30, we pushed on up to structure A. The sun had already left Stela 48, so we went up to the terrace of the beautiful monuments, where Frances took some more pictures.

After supper to celebrate the last evening we will all be together here at Calakmul, we opened our bottle of snake medicine, some six letter cognac, with which we toasted our most amazing luck here. We have a total of fifty-one Initial Series and one hundred three stelae, of which forty-one were found by the Carnegie Expedition.

April 24, Sunday

At 11:30 we were in saddles and turning our backs on Calakmul, which had yielded such splendid results to our efforts during the past fifteen days. In two hours we were back at Central Buenfils.

There was a truck in when we arrived but its magneto was out of order and the chauffeur seemed to be washing its different parts with gasoline. I got Gustav to help him, as the sooner the magneto was fixed, the sooner we could get started. I was just finishing paying off the workmen when it was reported that John, Karl, Jesus, and Laborio were in sight.

Frances brought me the serious news that Karl was down with a heavy attack of malaria which had struck him last night at the ruins and had arrived therefrom in a state of collapse. We all felt that he should be taken out to the coast as speedily as possible.

Meanwhile Gustav had been working on the magneto. He was able to get it to spark but so weakly that he said it could not be started by crank. The other White truck was down at kilometer 35, that is nine kilometers from Central Buenfils, with a broken steering gear. At 6:00 Don Manuel sent out an arriero with instructions to bring back the magneto from the broken White.

Preparations went forward for leaving sometime around midnight. Karl continued to be extremely ill.

John reported that the ruins they had visited had at least three Initial Series, one of 9.18.0.0.0 [A.D. 790], one of 9.19.0.0.0 [A.D. 810], and one of 10.1.0.0.0 [A.D. 849] or 10.2.0.0.0 [A.D. 869]. He reports the site as divided into two parts by a ravine up which the road runs. They only had time to map the group on the right side of the trail, locating twenty-three stelae, many·of which were fallen.

It was around midnight when I heard the engine of the truck exploding vigorously and realized that the magneto of the other truck must have arrived from kilometer 35 and had been changed to the truck which was to take us out. And so Sunday, the 24th, merged into Monday, the 25th, which from our point of view may well be dubbed "Blue Monday" because of its contretemps and discomforts.

April 25, Monday

There were to be nineteen people going out, plus our baggage and a single layer of blocks of chicle on the floor of the truck to make it ride easier. The loading of all our baggage and leaving an even, only fairly comfortable place for us at the front of the truck was no light job. The moon had been up about an hour by midnight, and Gustav, with his valuable knowledge of lashing, cables, and knots, undertook to see that this was done properly. Experience had shown us on the way in that what was not lashed to the sides of the truck slid all over it. The truck hands had already laid down one layer of chicle blocks at the rear and on top of this were placed kyacks and gasoline boxes. Forward the jute bags containing the saddles and the chairs were lashed to the right side, and with pillows and bags of blankets against the south side as a brace, we lay on the layer of chicle.

Frances was forward, then me, then Karl, then John, and Gustav last, facing in the opposite direction. Behind Gustav, jammed together on the boxes sat the seven Tuxpenos and Demetrio, holding a simian infant, Simonita.

Although we had been up at 1:00, breakfasted and finished packing hammocks and so on, it was 4:15 by my watch when we finally snorted out of the area enclosed by the principal houses and sheds at Central Buenfils. Goodbyes were said to Don Manuel Osorno. Karl had been helped out to the car and up into his own particular place in the box of sardines, because he is our largest fish. We had all wiggled ourselves into more or less comfortable positions.

It became apparent at once that we were going to ride much more easily on the return trip than we had in coming in. This was due to several different causes. First, because with the extra stratum of chicle on the bottom of the truck and the eight extra people, we were much more heavily loaded and the car rode correspondingly more easily. Second, because our chauffeur was obviously a much more careful driver than the one we had coming in. He did not rush at the hills, and he certainly eased us over the rocks and other rough places with greater skill. Finally, the road itself, having had no rain to speak of since we had passed over it more than a fortnight before, was in better condition. All combined to make the riding easier, for which I was very glad for Karl's sake. Don Manuel estimated that it would take us seven hours to make the trip to Río Desempeño, but I saw that at the rate we were leaving the kilometers behind us, it was going to take more than eight hours. At kilometer 35 we passed the broken down truck and only paused long enough for the chauffeur to get some things out of its tool box.

About 11:30 when we had just five more miles to go, the steering rod broke and there we were. Fortunately for us, the accident happened in a patch of high forest and not in one of the blazing hot akalches, otherwise we would have suffered from the heat much more. Our chauffeurs were in no doubt as to what the accident meant: abandonment of the truck and hoofing it into Río Desempeño. I told the Tuxpenos to leave their baggage, but that they also should walk.

I wrote a letter to the local manager at Río Desempeño asking him to send out three arrias of pack animals and seven riding animals just as soon as he could as I had a sick man with me and wanted to get him out of the bush at once. The supercargo took this letter with him, setting out with the rest of the auto crew and the Tuxpenos at 11:45.

I calculated that it would take them two hours to walk in, and allowing three-fourths of an hour to get the mules ready, they ought to be started back by half after two, reaching us no later than 4:30. Allowing half an hour for loading our baggage on them, we ought to be starting on toward Río

Desempeño about 5:00. These calculations of mine proved to be too optimistic by about four to five hours.

The only boy who stayed behind with us was Demetrio, who said that a walk of two hours at this time of day would kill Simonita without a doubt. He elected to stay with us until succour should come.

When we were alone, our first care was for Karl. Tarsisio, Gustav, and Demetrio cleared a place between some trees on the shady side of the road, and here his hammock and mosquito bar were hung. We helped him out of the car and into the hammock where he could be more comfortable.

Frances put Arturo to getting a lunch, which we ate on a piece of canvas stretched across the trail. I had Frances's hammock hung. After lunch she and I took our siesta in it, while Gustav and John slept on a ground cloth and Tarsisio, Arturo, and Demetrio in the truck.

It was hot and sticky even in the shade. What with our anxiety over Karl, none of us enjoyed our siesta very much. Karl's fever continued high, and he vomited occasionally. We kept him filled with quinine, twenty grains at a time, so that he was deaf from the ringing of the drug in his ears.

After siesta someone thought of bridge. Gustav got the cards, and we played on the ground on a piece of canvas. We played until a youth showed up from Río Desempeño with a letter from Don Manuel Bolivar which was a kind of lament. There were no carts in El Rio, all being at Tanche where they were hauling chicle and from where they were expected about 3:00 in the morning. In place of carts, *after sunset* when the plague of flies had abated somewhat, he would send several arrias to bring us in.

This meant another long wait, but there was no help for it, so inditing another letter to him urging him earnestly, despairingly not to fail me in my dire need, and again stressing the imperative necessity of getting Karl out of the bush tonight, I despatched this second letter by the young Belizano, who promised to have it in Don Manuel's hands in another hour.

By this time it was about 4:30. It was evident we were going to have to unload the truck, which Gustav had loaded so carefully twelve hours before, but it seemed wisest to get this done before nightfall. Then Frances had Arturo prepare a puree of pea after a recipe of her own, and this was delicious. Together with cherries, cheese spread, and Educator crackers, we had supper before it got dark.

After supper there was nothing further to do until the mules from El Rio arrived. We gave Karl a little soda to settle his stomach, twenty grains more quinine, some hot tea, and some puree. Then by the light of two flashlights hung at diagonal corners of our improvised table, two gasoline boxes, we again played auction. As quickly as night fell in the forest, the mosquitoes began to sing. We lowered Karl's pabellon so as to keep him from being bitten.

At 8:00 we heard a tramping of feet in the forest toward the north, and soon an arriero came in with his arria, four animals with packs for cargo and one without a pack for a saddle animal. He reported two other arrieros were following with seven more pack animals and five more riding animals. We selected the most urgent of our baggage and with John assisting the arriero, these were loaded on to the backs of the cargo animals. The single saddle animal brought by the first arriero was saddled with Karl's saddle but held until we were ready to leave.

The wall-eyed arriero with the first four pack animals must have got off for El Rio about 9:15. It was decided that with Demetrio as a guide, leading the way on foot, Frances, Karl, Tarsisio, and I would go next. Gustav and John were going to see that everything else went on the remaining eleven pack animals and that nothing was left behind. It transpired then that the riding animals were incomplete in number. The first arriero had brought one which was already saddled with Karl's saddle. The second and third arrieros had started from El Rio with only five extra riding animals and had managed to lose one in the dark, or two less than we needed. In the face of this condition, tired as they were, Gustav and John walked.

We thought we could make the trip in two hours. It was delightful riding in the cool of the night, and if we could only be sure we were on the right trail, there was nothing to worry about. Demetrio knew the way and since Karl was standing the ride in great shape, I really was not concerned.

About an hour out the road forked. We took the right road, which Demetrio said was a short cut. I thought this must be the correct road too because later Demetrio found on it the raincoat of the wall-eyed arriero, which he must have dropped as he went ahead of us. Later just about the time I began to fear we were lost, we came back into the main road. Here the ruts worn by the trucks could be clearly traced.

Fireflies kept deceiving us though as to the lights of Río Desempeño. We could see one ahead in the road, only to have it flicker out as we approached it. At 11:25 we crossed an enormous milpa which had been burned about a week ago. It gave the effect of passing through some city, as lights were glowing everywhere, these the still burning remains of fallen trees and stumps. It was quite uncanny to come upon this great phantom city in the dark and to know that none of those merry lights shone from some home.

We knew by the signs of this milpa that we must be nearly there. Meantime I had picked out the Great Dipper and the North Star and so knew we were following the right direction. Finally at 11:35, two hours and five minutes after leaving the truck, Demetrio caught sight of a fixed light. We knew we had arrived.

SELECTED RELATED READINGS

Brainerd, George W.
1954 *The Maya Civilization.* Southwest Museum, Los Angeles, Calif.

Coe, Michael D.
1966 *The Maya.* Frederick A. Prager, New York

Gann, T.W.F.
1918 *The Maya Indians of Southern Yucatan and Northern British Honduras.* Smithsonian Institution, Bureau of American Ethnology, Bulletin 64. Washington, D.C.

Lothrop, Samuel K.
1924 *Tulum: An Archaeological Study of the East Coast of Yucatan.* Carnegie Institution of Washington, Publication 335. Washington, D.C.

Morley, Sylvanus G.
1915 *An Introduction to the Study of Maya Hieroglyphics.* Smithsonian Institution, Bureau of American Ethnology, Bulletin 57. Washington, D.C.
1938 *The Inscriptions of Peten.* 5 vols. Carnegie Institution of Washington, Publication 437. Washington, D.C.

Morley, Sylvanus G. and George W. Brainerd
1956 *The Ancient Maya.* Stanford University Press, Stanford, California.

Proskouriakoff, Tatiana
1946 *An Album of Maya Architecture.* Carnegie Institution of Washington, Publication 558. Washington, D.C.
1950 *A Study of Classic Maya Sculpture.* Carnegie Institution of Washington, Publication 593. Washington, D.C.

Spinden, Herbert J.
1913 *A Study of Maya Art.* Peabody Museum of American Archaeology and Ethnology, Memoir, v. 6. Cambridge, Massachusetts.

Stephens, John L.
1841 *Incidents of Travel in Central America, Chiapas, and Yucatan.* 2 vols. Harper and Bros., New York.
1843 *Incidents of Travel in Yucatan.* 2 vols. Harper and Bros., New York.

Thompson, J. Eric S.

   1950   *Maya Hieroglyphic Writing: An Introduction.* Carnegie Institution
          of Washington, Publication 589. Washington, D.C.

   1954   *The Rise and Fall of Maya Civilization.* University of Oklahoma
          Press, Norman, Oklahoma.

Tozzer, Alfred M.

   1941   *Landa's Relación de las Cosas de Yucatan.* Peabody Museum of
          American Archaeology and Ethnology, Papers, v. 18. Cambridge,
          Massachusetts.

GLOSSARY

aguada – reservoir or water hole

akalche – area of low bush

alcalde – mayor

aparejo – harness

arria – drove of horses or mules

arriero – muleteer

atole – gruel

bajo – low lying ground

baktun – 144,000 days in Maya calendric system

bejuco – liana

bush – dense growth of saplings and brushwood where there is insufficient ground moisture to carry larger trees through dry season. Morley also calls the rain forest of the Petén the bush.

camino real – royal road, main trail

cenote – natural "well" formed when limestone surface collapses exposing underground water, characteristic of northern Yucatan peninsula

Chac Mool – Toltec inspired sculptured reclining male figure holding a basin on its stomach

champa – camp shelter

chicle – sap used for making chewing gum

chiclero – gatherer of chicle

chultún – water reservoir underground

cilantro – coriander, an herb

cuadrilla – force of workers

entrada – entrance

galerones – large rooms or corridors; name locally applied to temporary shelters built at camping places

garrapata – tick

Glyph G – usually in seventh position in Initial Series; refers to one of nine gods who was patron of specific day of Maya chronological era of the Initial Series in question

guano – kind of palm tree

henequen – sisal hemp, product of agave plant

hotun – five years in Maya calendric system

Initial Series – record of dates from beginning of Maya calendar system, usually five glyphs

jato – clearing and household farm

jornada – journey, usually of a day's length

katun – 7,200 days, approximately twenty years, in Maya calendric system

kin – one day in Maya calendric system

lahuntun – approximately ten years in Maya

lamina – sheet metal

machete – cutlass

milpa – farm plot

monte – mountain

montería – area of mahogany cutting operations

mozo – servant

mulada – mule train

pabellon – mosquito net

paraje (parage) – stopping place

patacho – mule train

picado – rough trail

quintal – hundredweight

ramon – bread nut tree, *Brosimum alicastrum Sw.*, apparently planted by ancient Maya and now cover many Classic period sites

ramonal – grove of bread nut trees, used for feed for pack animals

sapote (zapote) – tropical American tree, sapota, which bears edible fruit

Secondary Series – Maya dates derived from the Initial Series by either addition or subtraction, a calendar correction formula to bring the calendar year into accord with the tropical year

Short Count – abbreviated system used in the Postclassic period which reduced the number of necessary glyphs but also reduced accuracy to 256 years

stela – stone shaft raised as a marker to commemorate the passing of various periods of time and perhaps to record historical events

Supplementary Series – moon count; usually six glyphs after the Initial Series which presumably give lunar information about the day in question

tamagus (tamagás) – very poisonous Central American snake

tlachtli – Aztec name for prehistoric Middle American ball game played on ceremonial occasions

tun – 18 uinals or 360 days in Maya calendric system

uinal – 20 kins or days in Maya calendric system

volancoche – rough-riding wheeled coach

zacate – grass